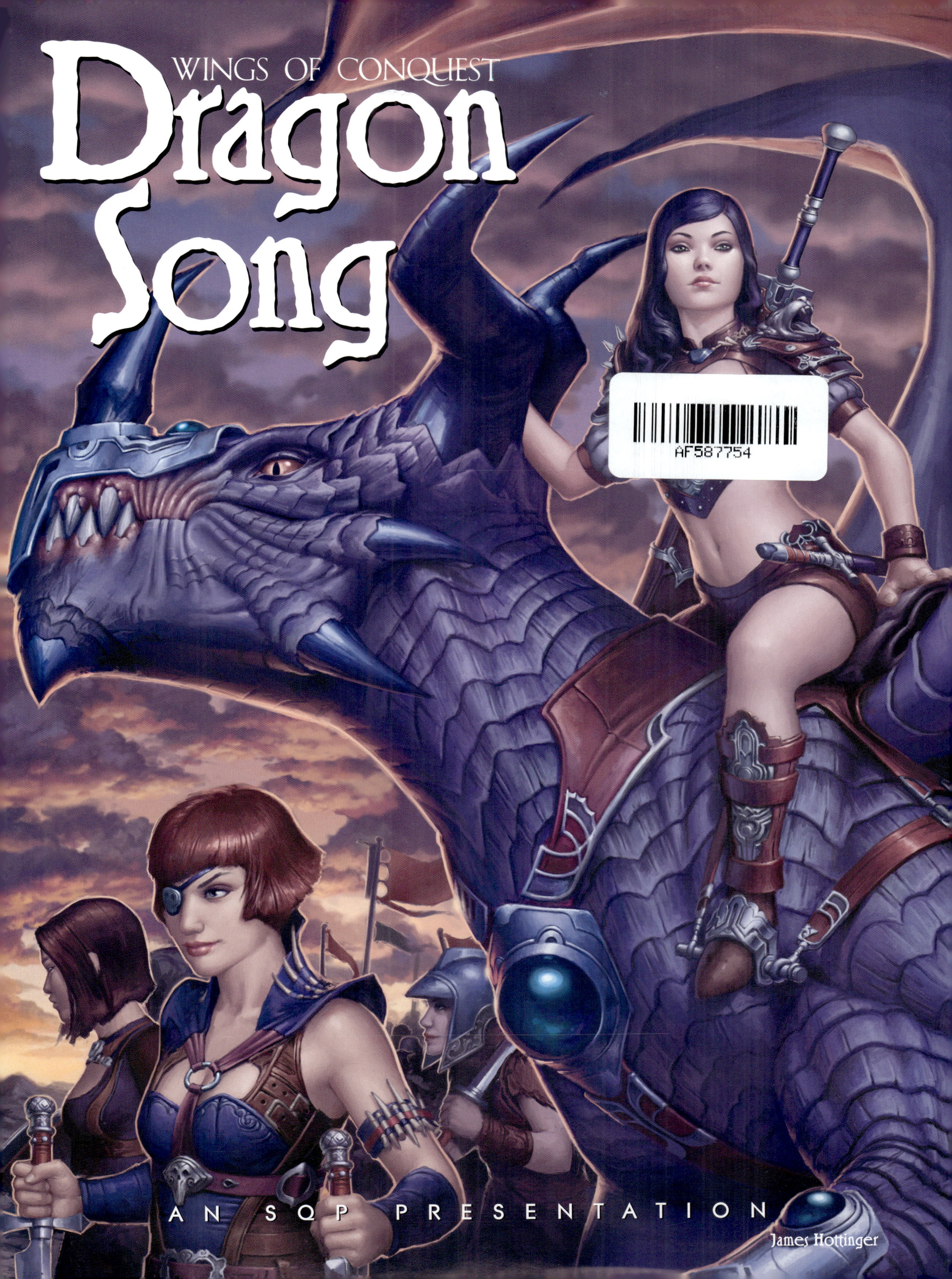
WINGS OF CONQUEST
Dragon Song
AF587754
AN SQP PRESENTATION
James Hottinger

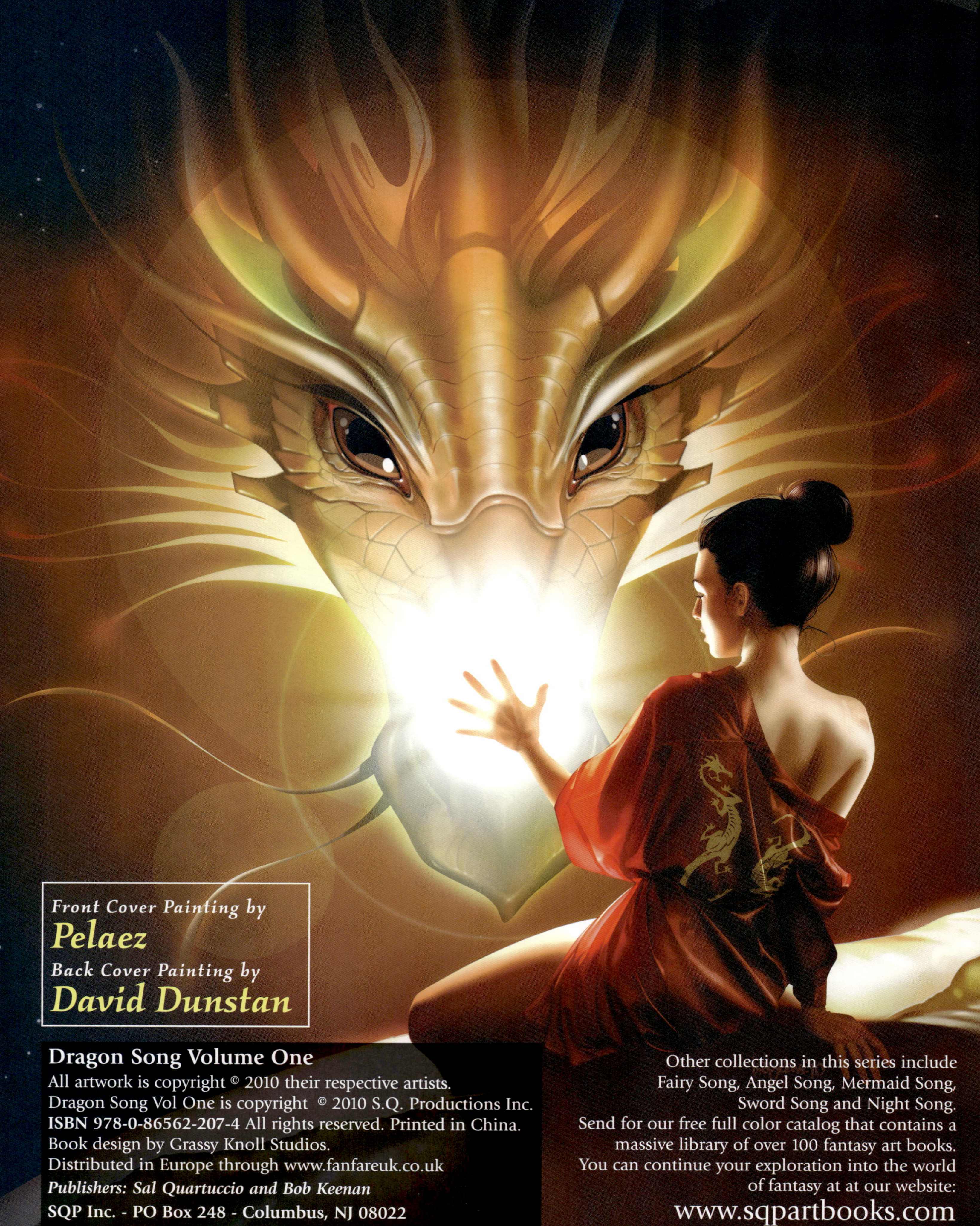

Front Cover Painting by
Pelaez
Back Cover Painting by
David Dunstan

Dragon Song Volume One

ISBN 978-0-86562-207-4 All rights reserved. Printed in China.
Book design by Grassy Knoll Studios.
Distributed in Europe through www.fanfareuk.co.uk
Publishers: Sal Quartuccio and Bob Keenan
SQP Inc. - PO Box 248 - Columbus, NJ 08022

David Dunstan

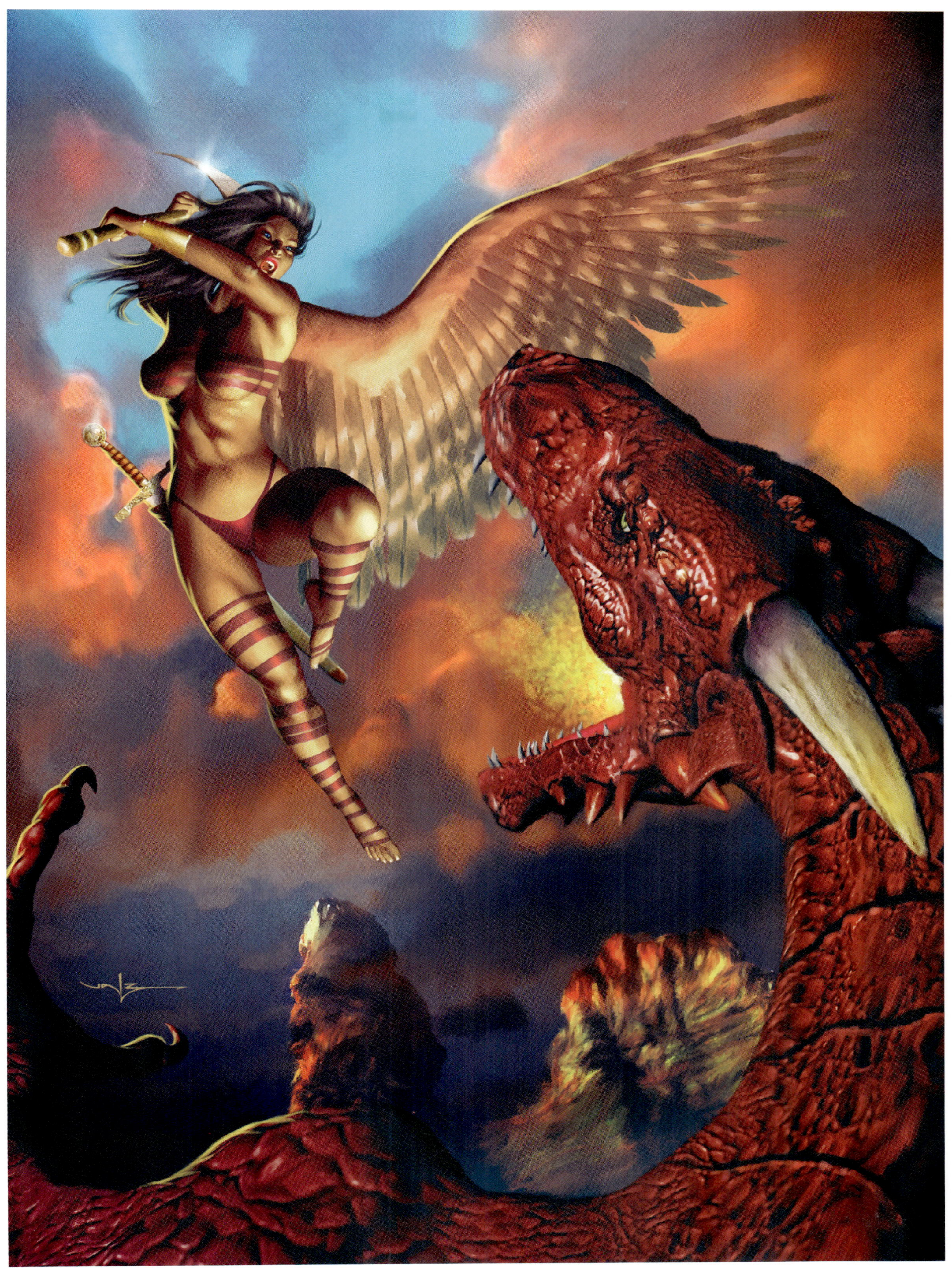

Carlos Valenzuela

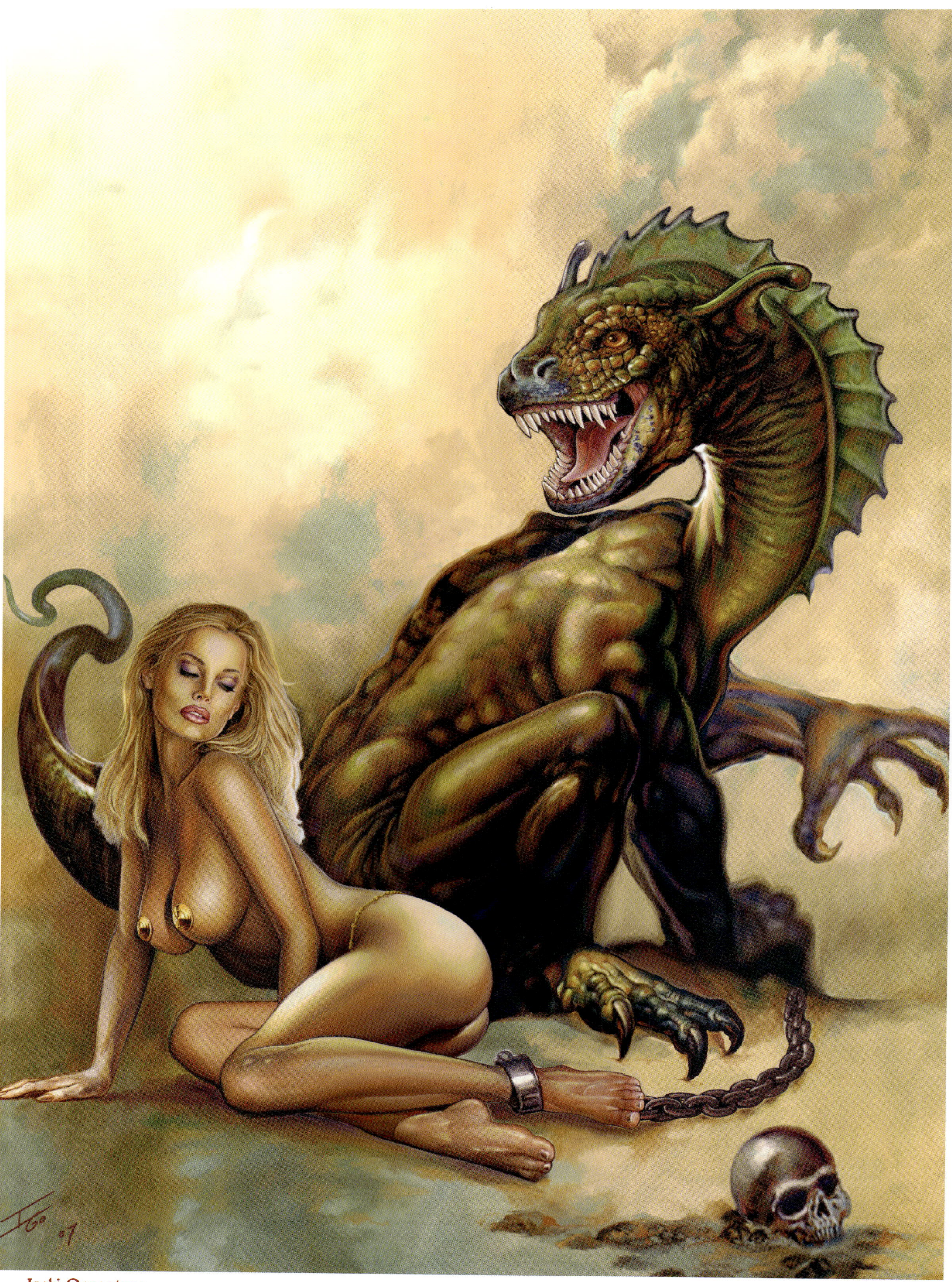

Inaki Ormaetxea

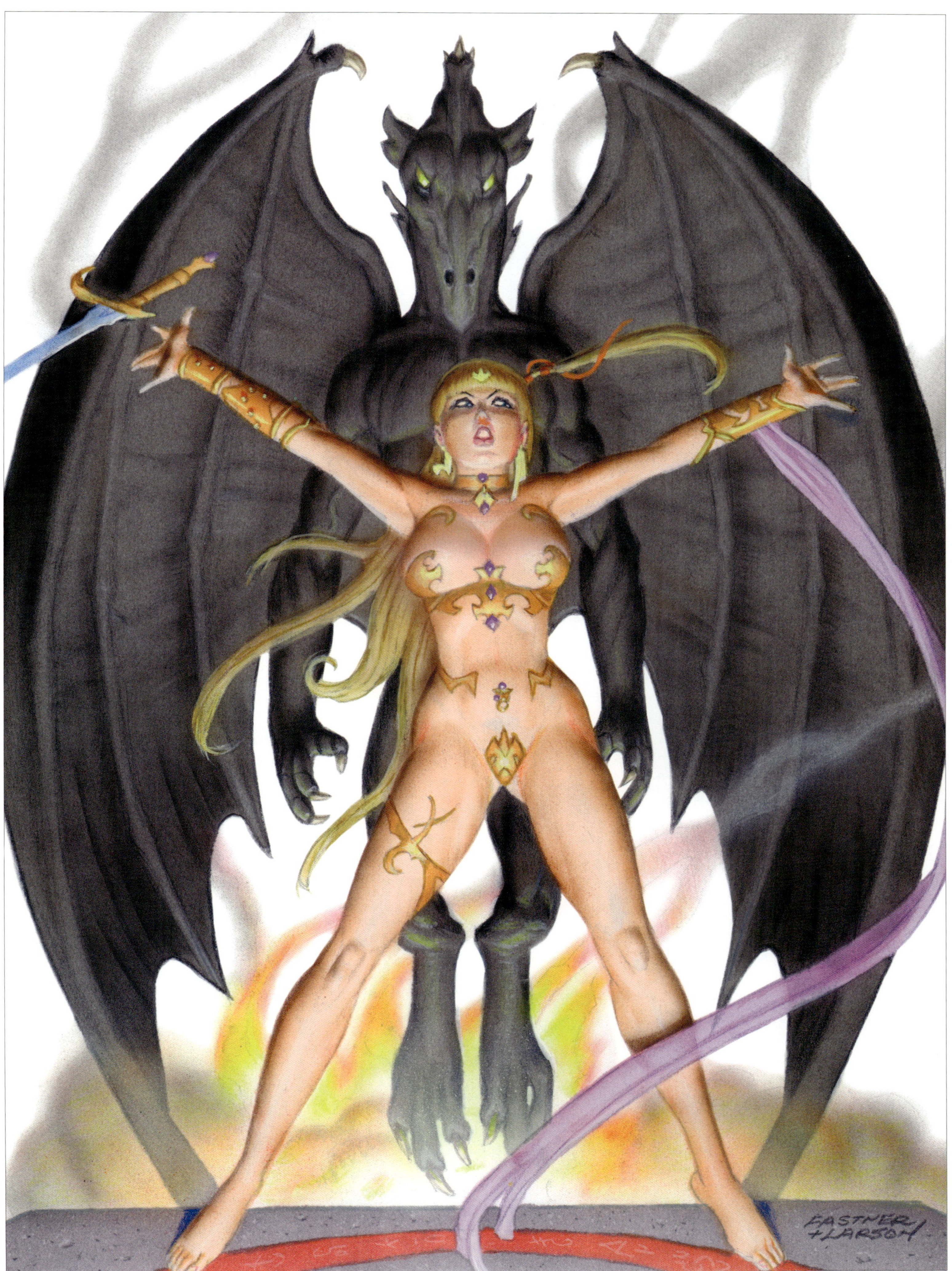

Steve Fastner & Rich Larson

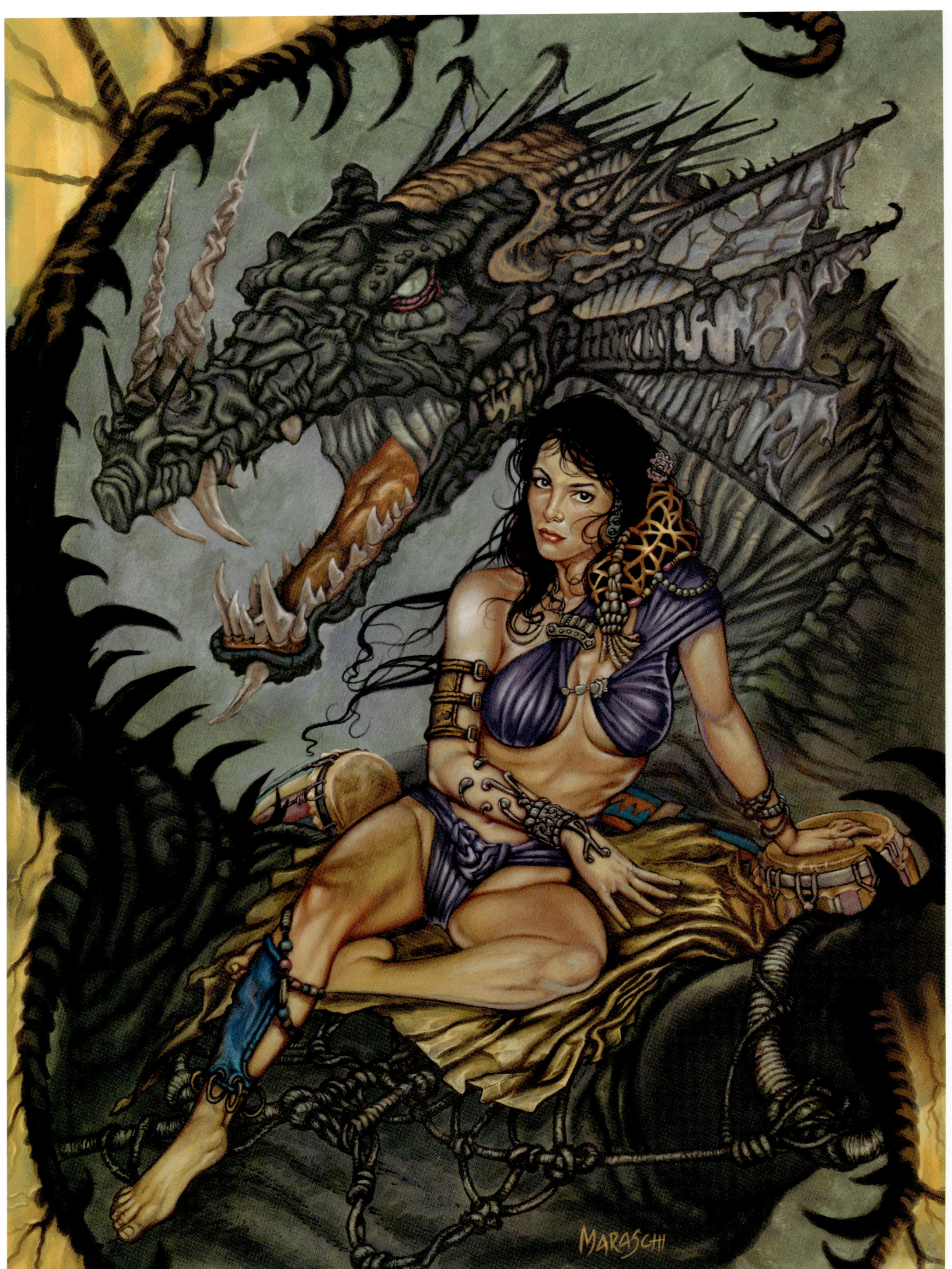

Anibal Maraschi

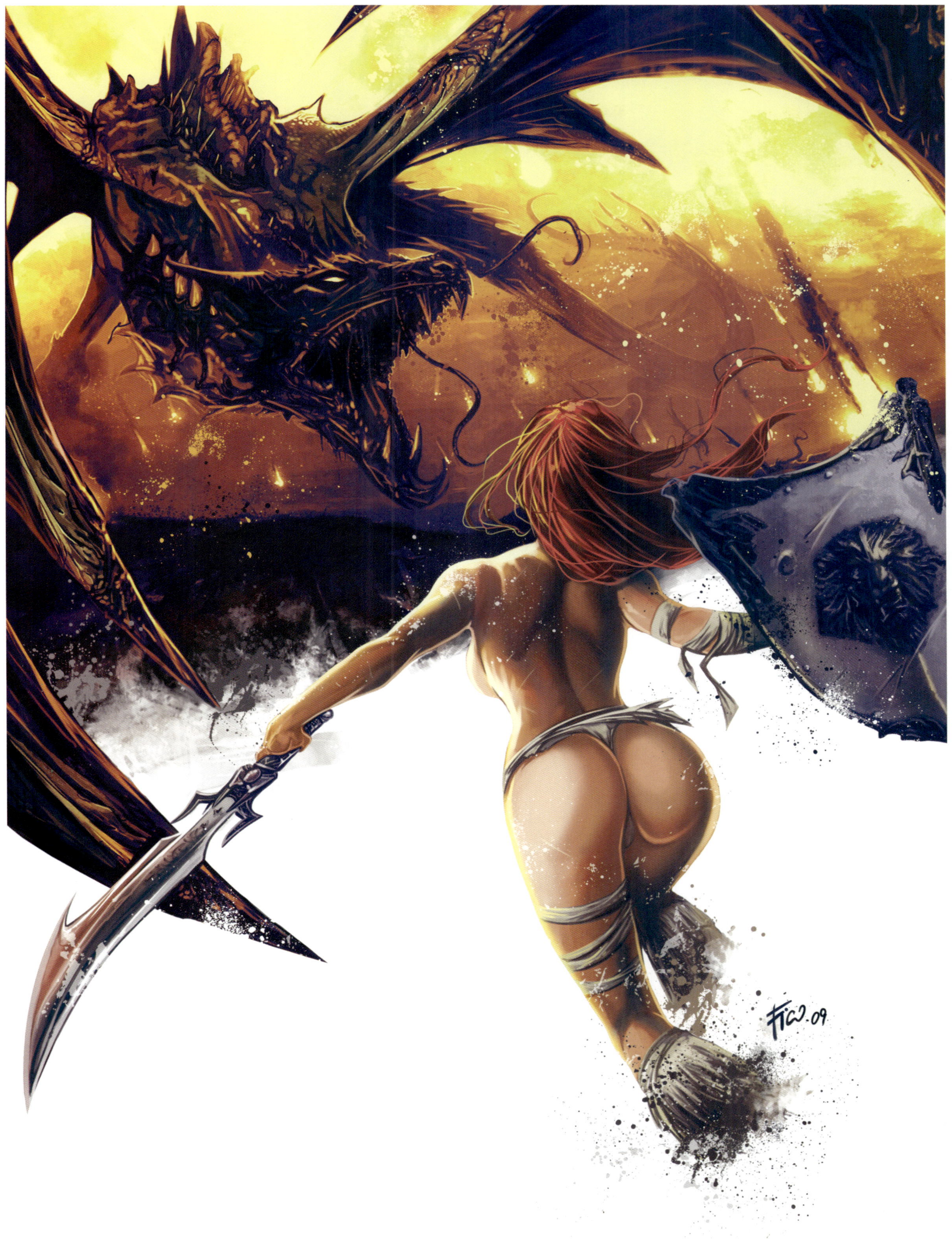

Federico Ossio

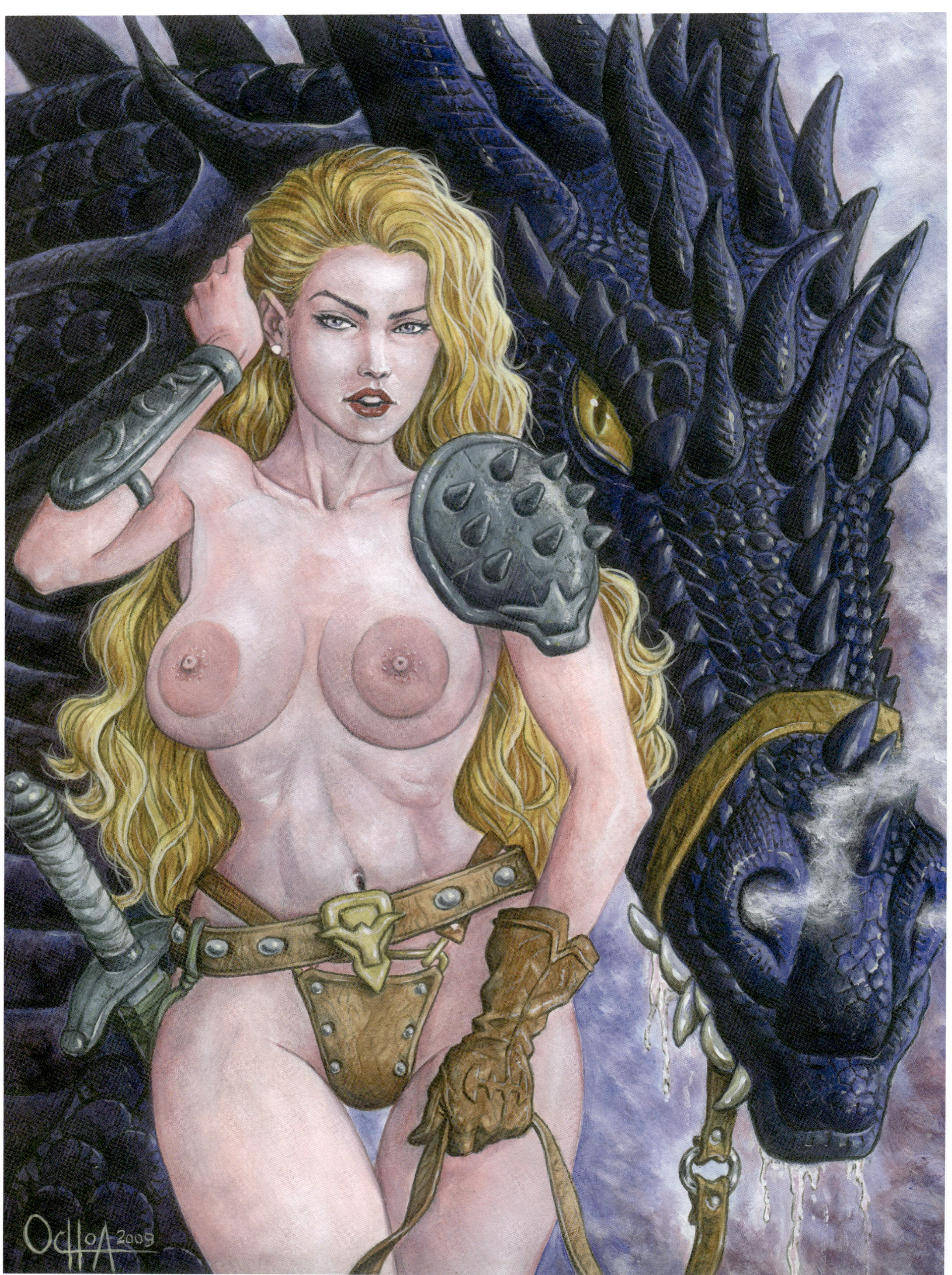

Percy Ochoa

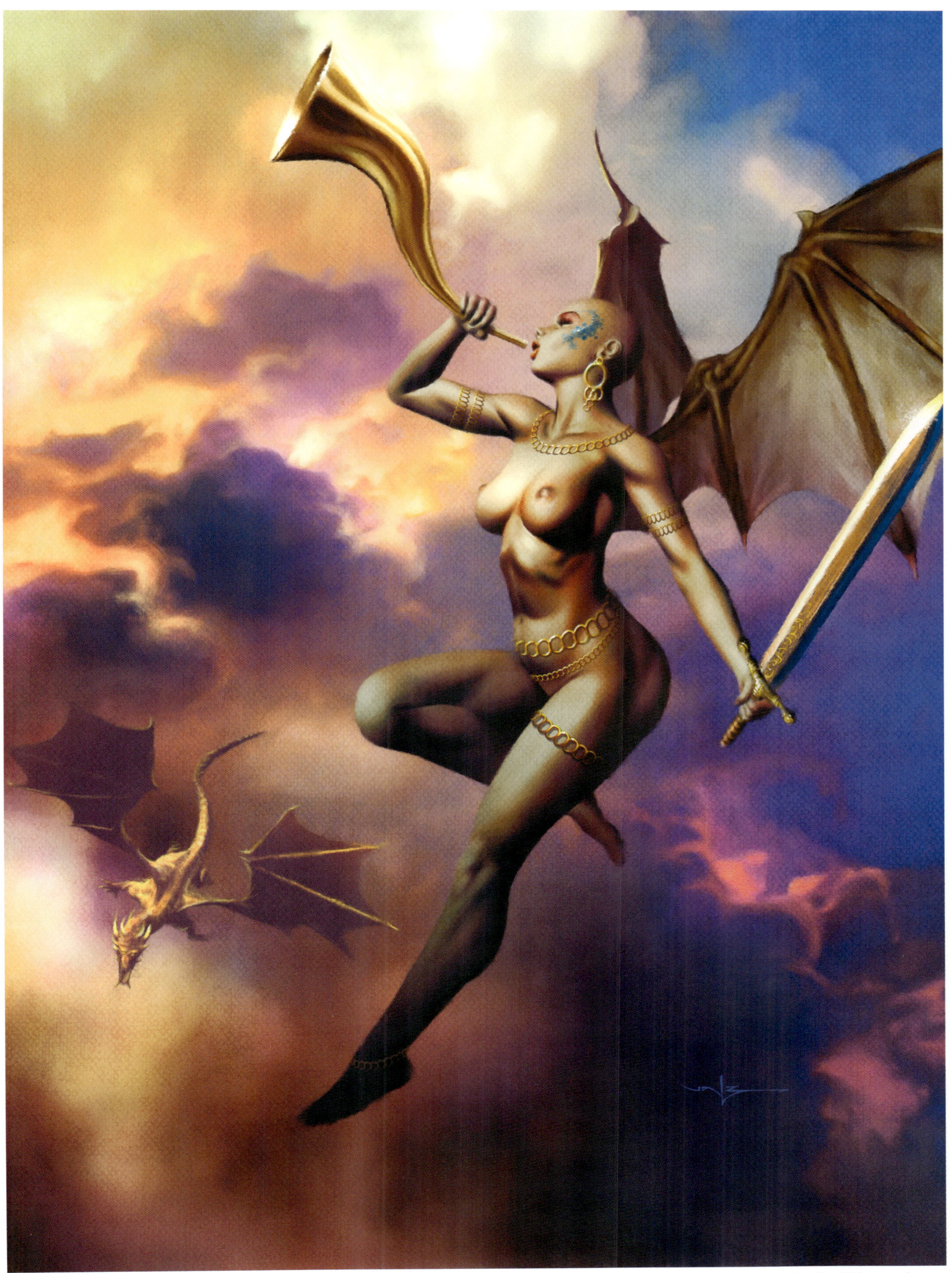

Carlos Valenzuela

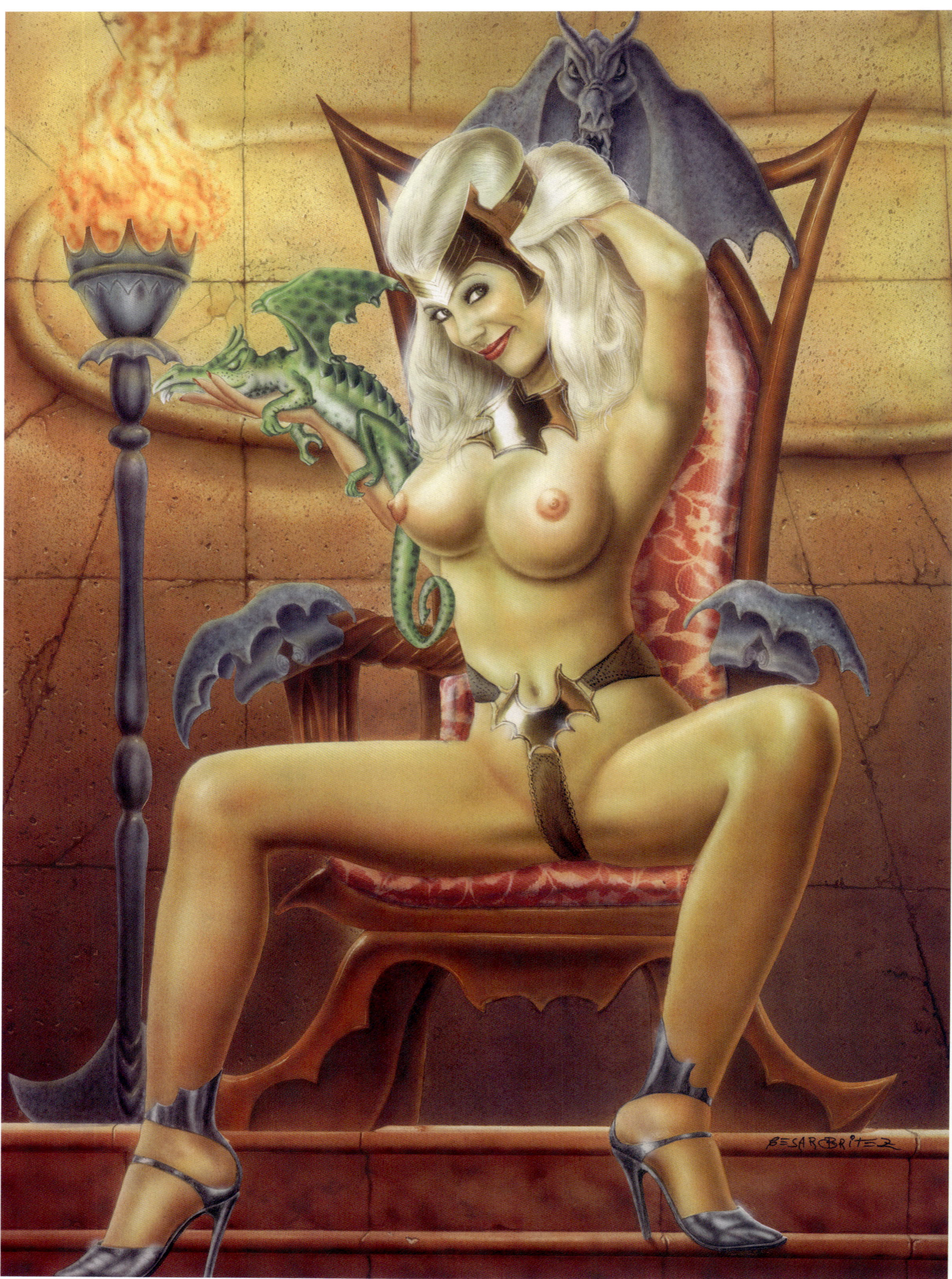

Cesar Britez

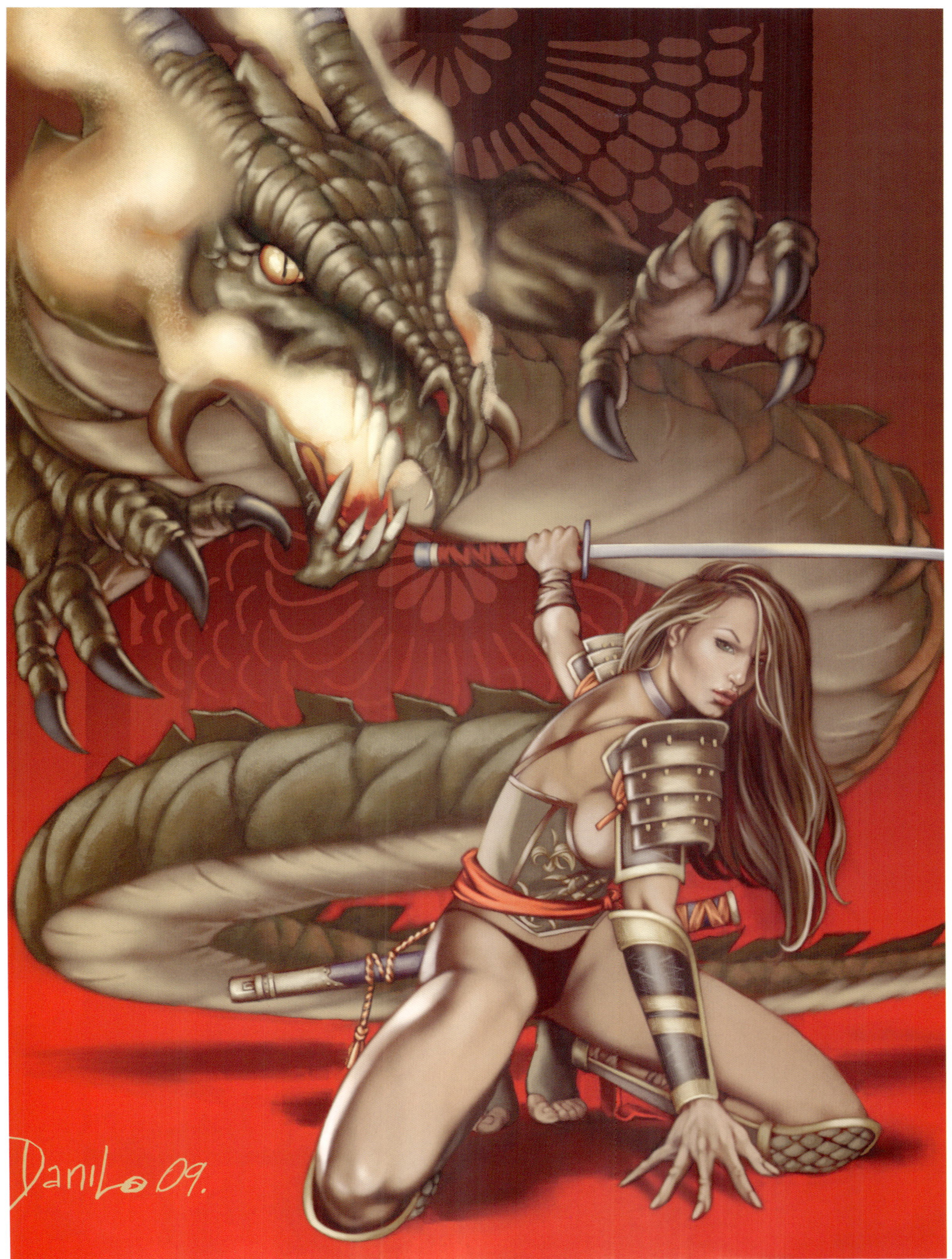

Danilo Guida

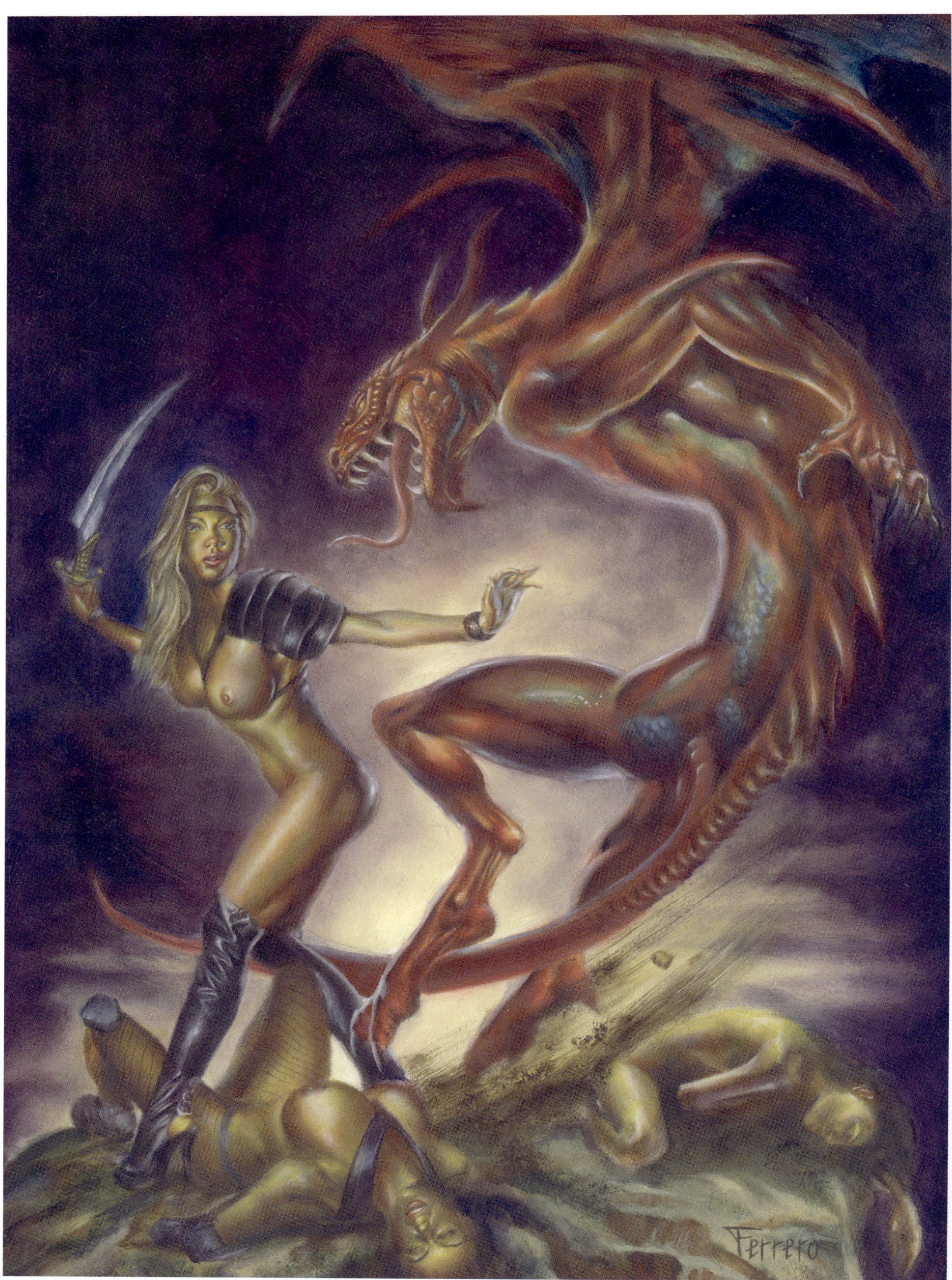

Alejandro Ferrero

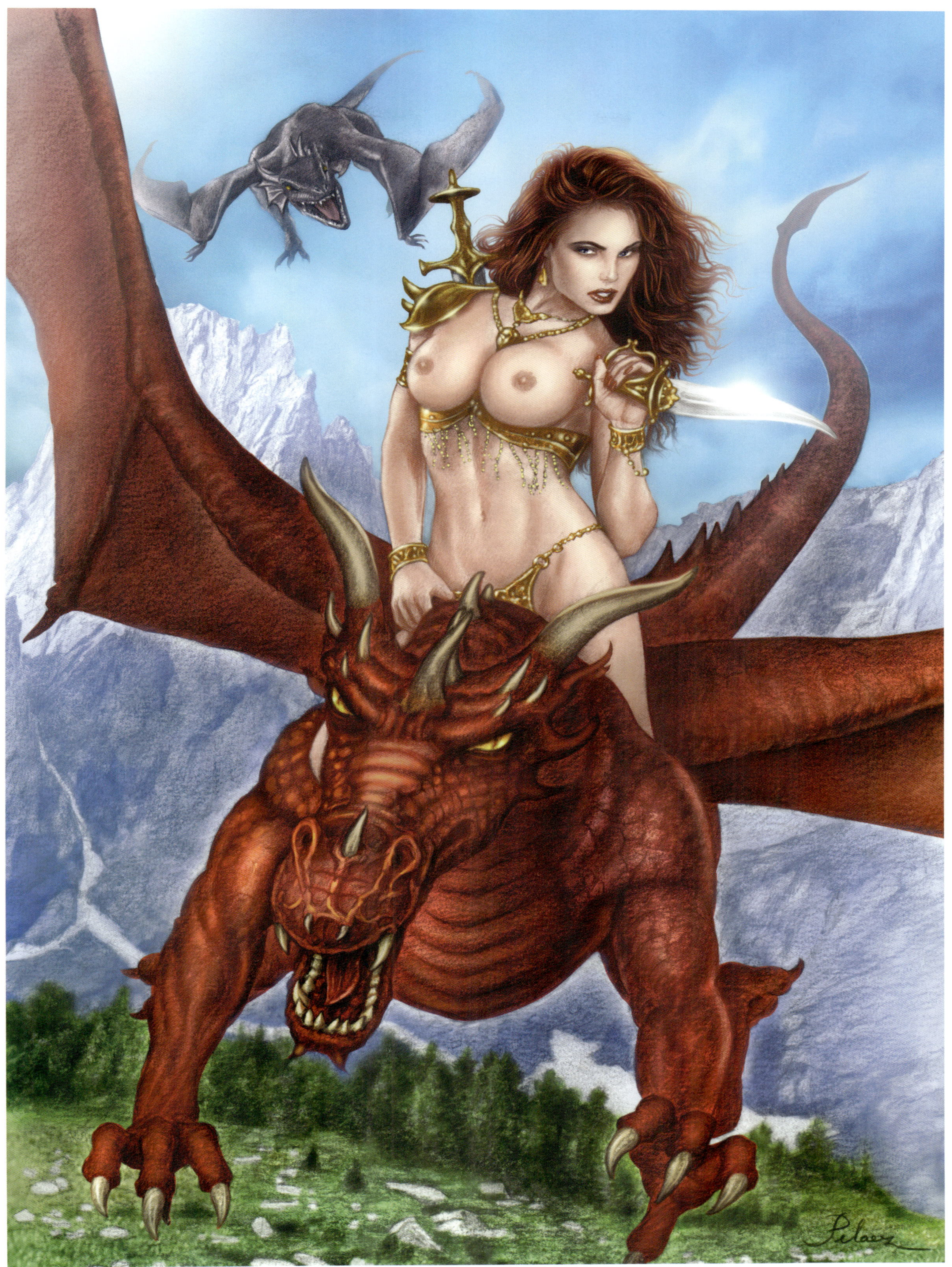

Pelaez/Jose Cano

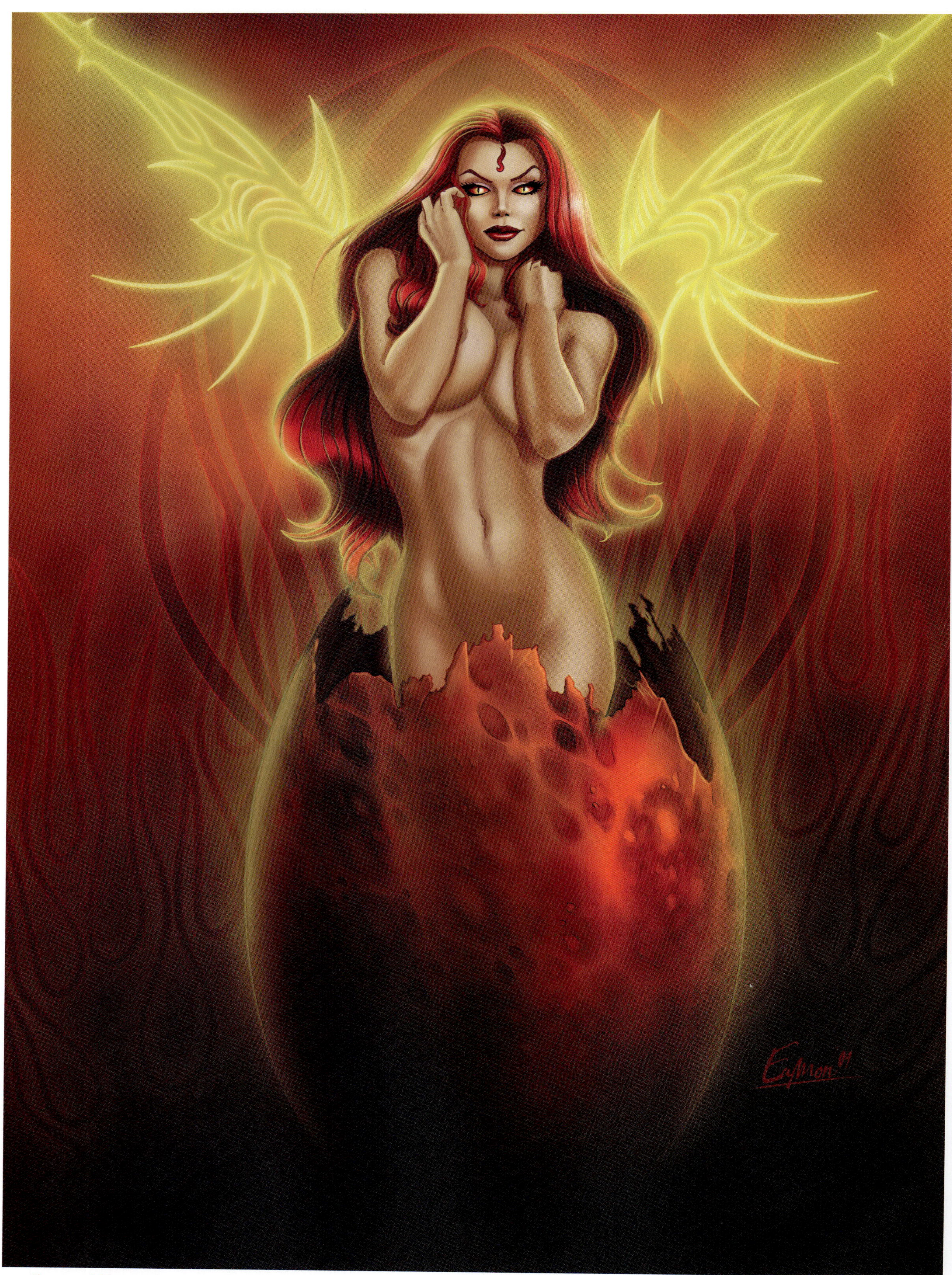

Eamon O'Donoghue

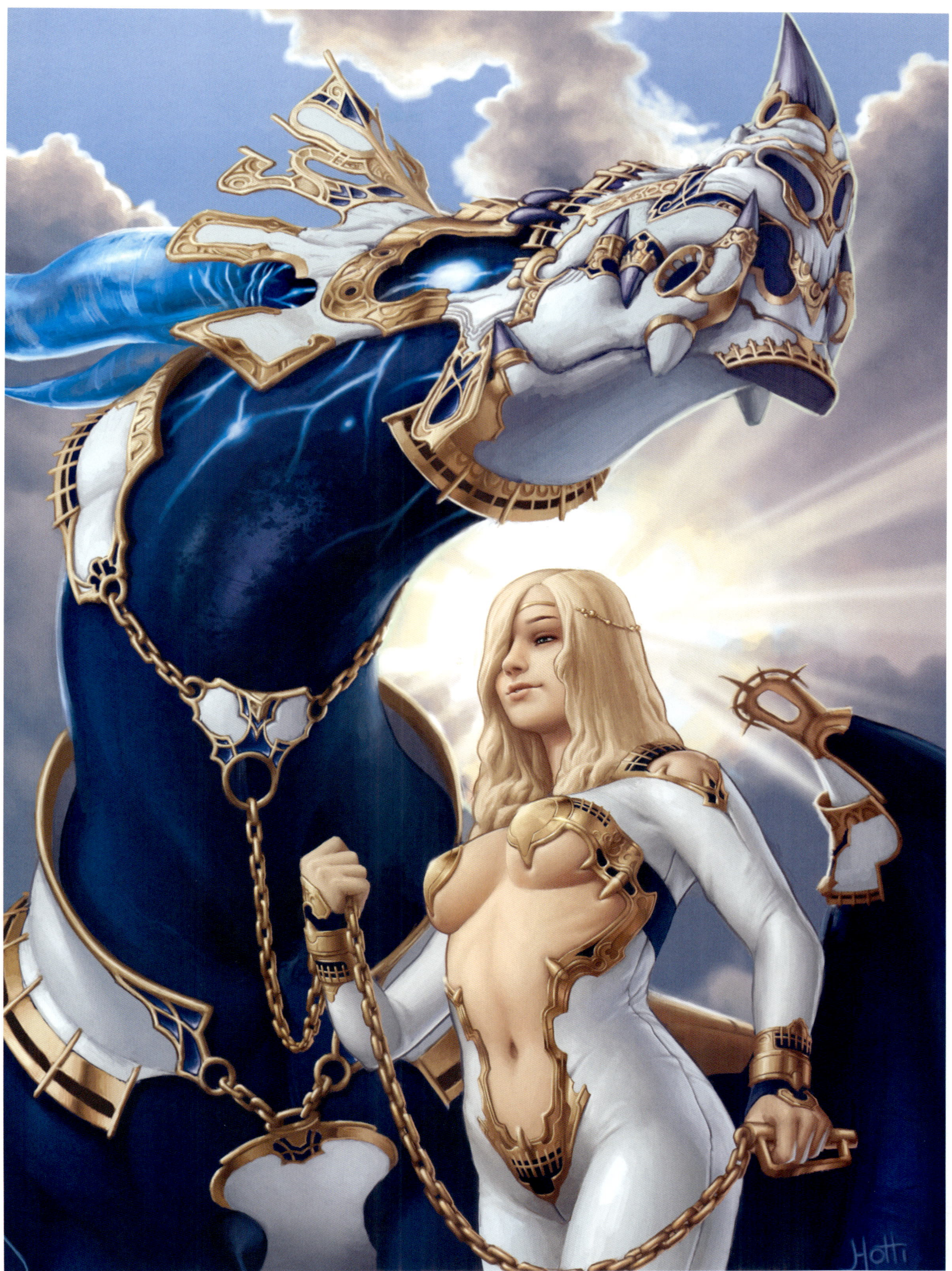

James Hottinger

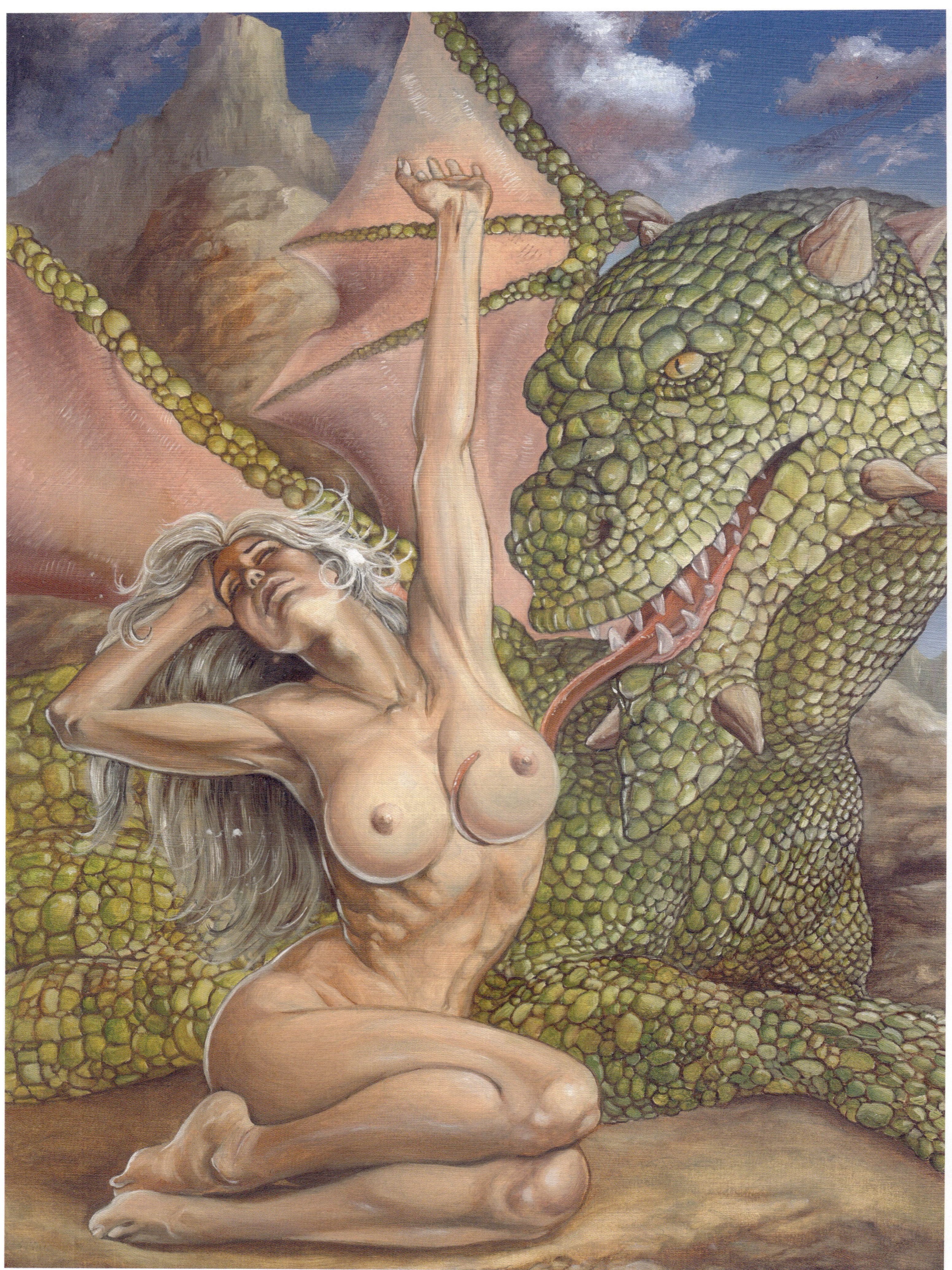

Diego Florio

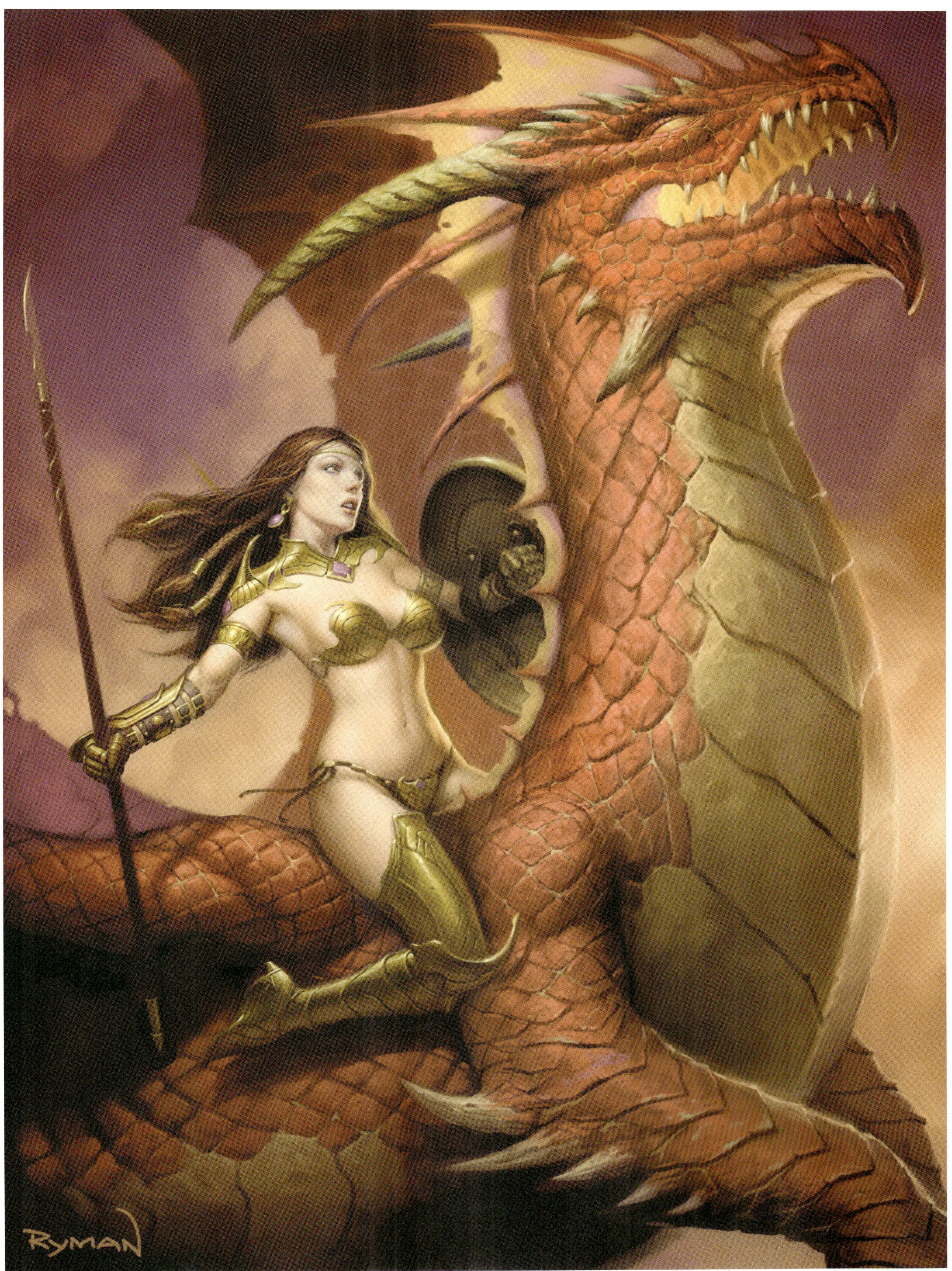

James Ryman

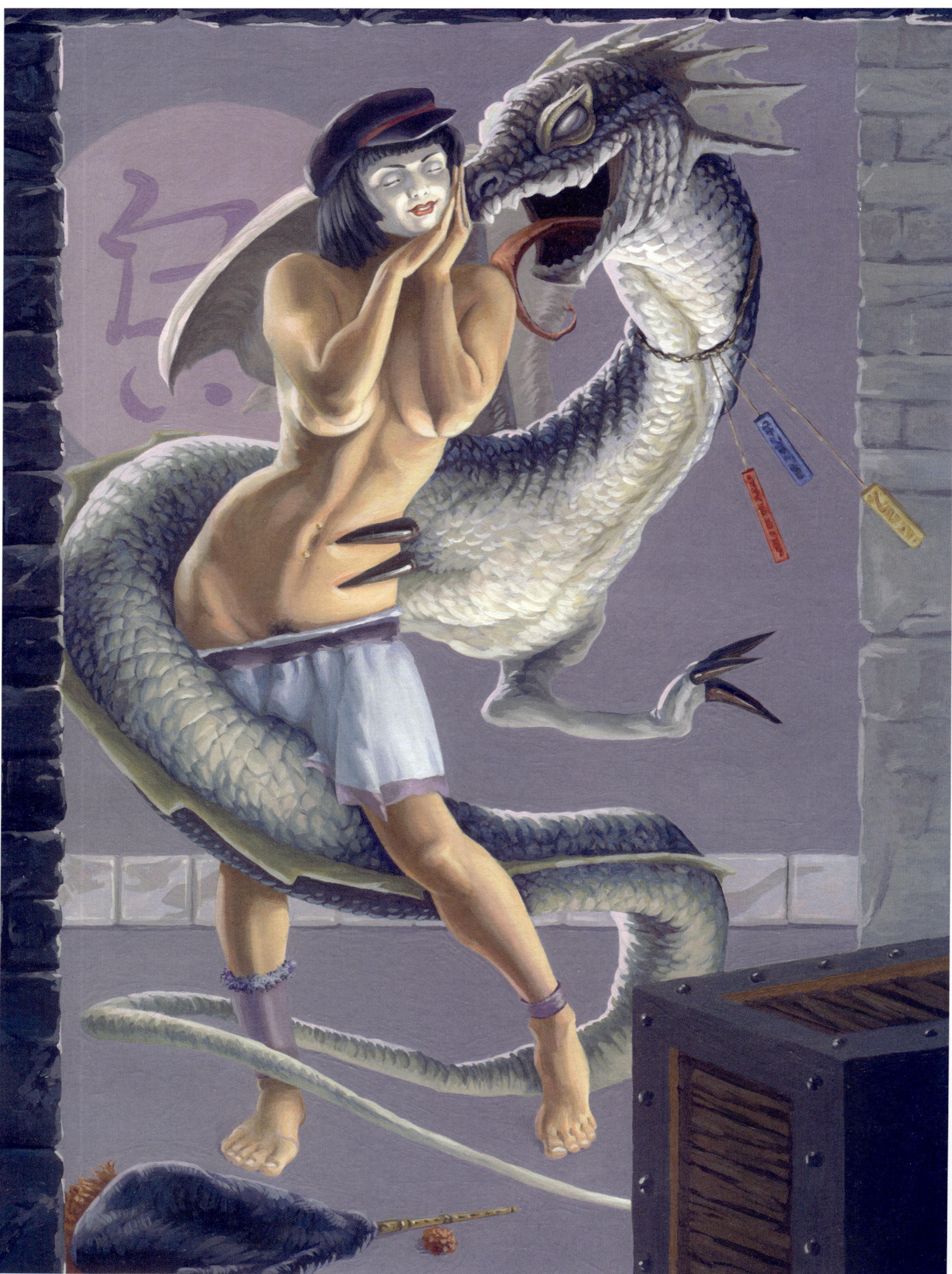

Diego Cirulli

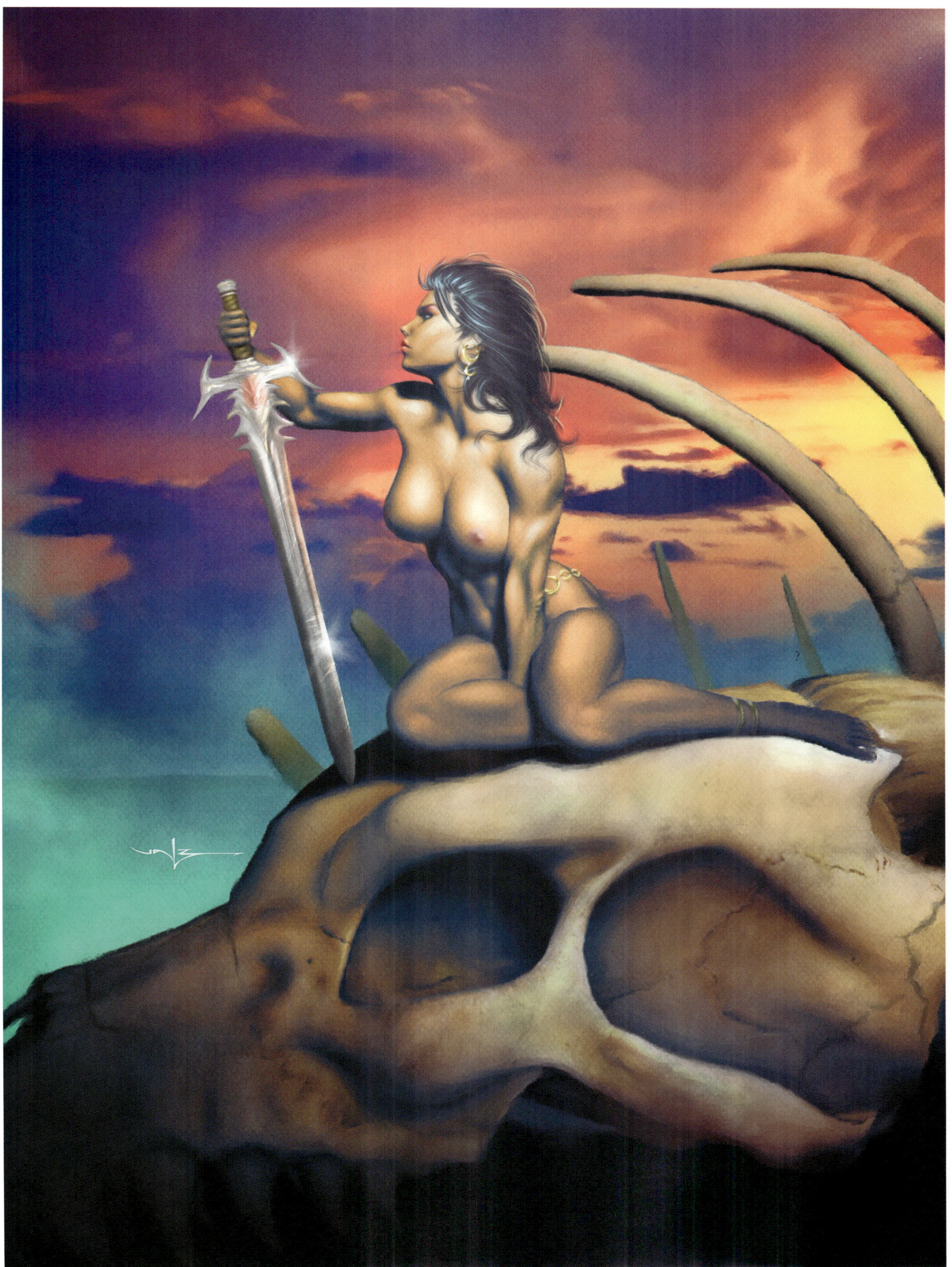

Carlos Valenzuela

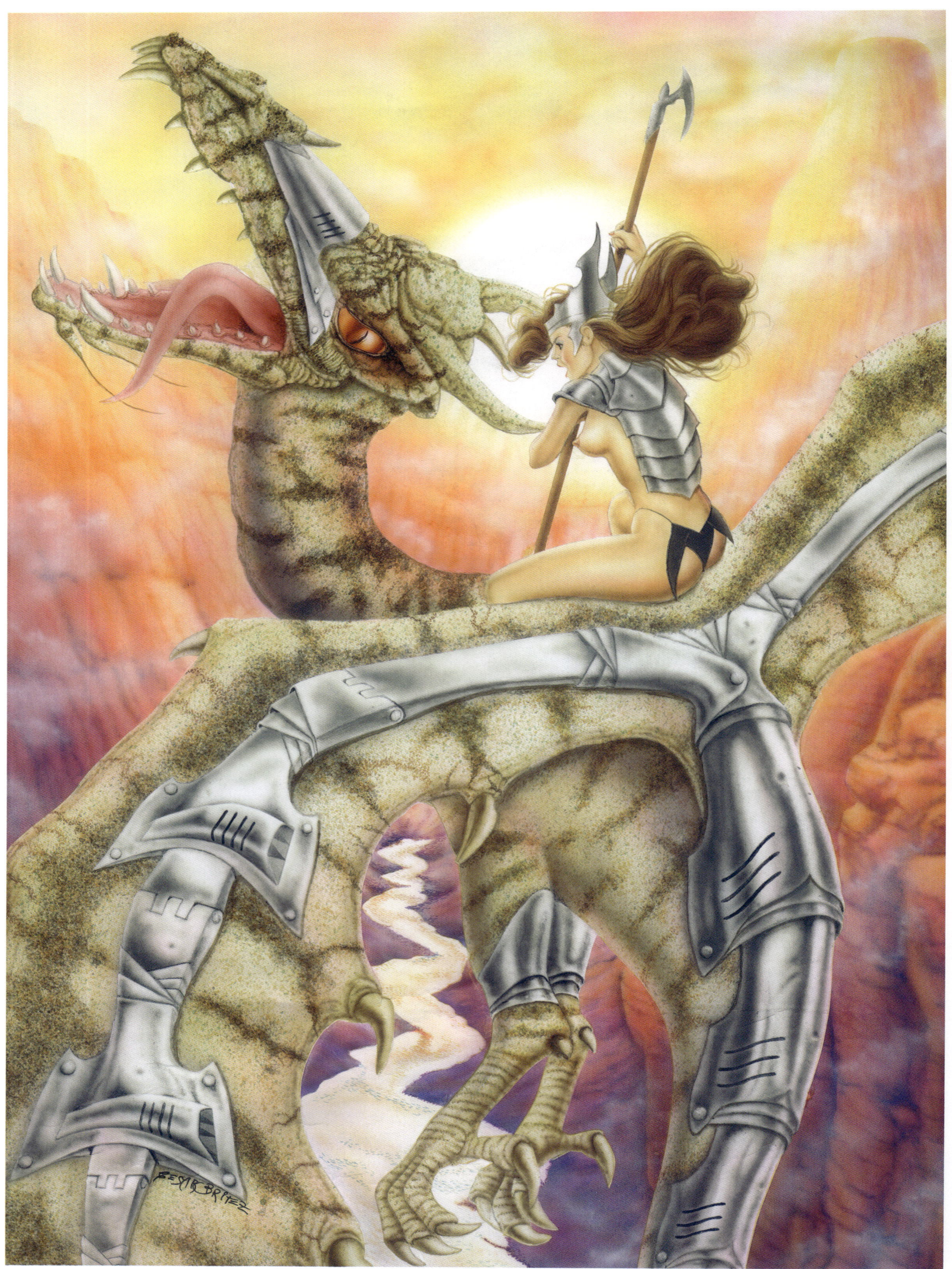

Cesar Britez

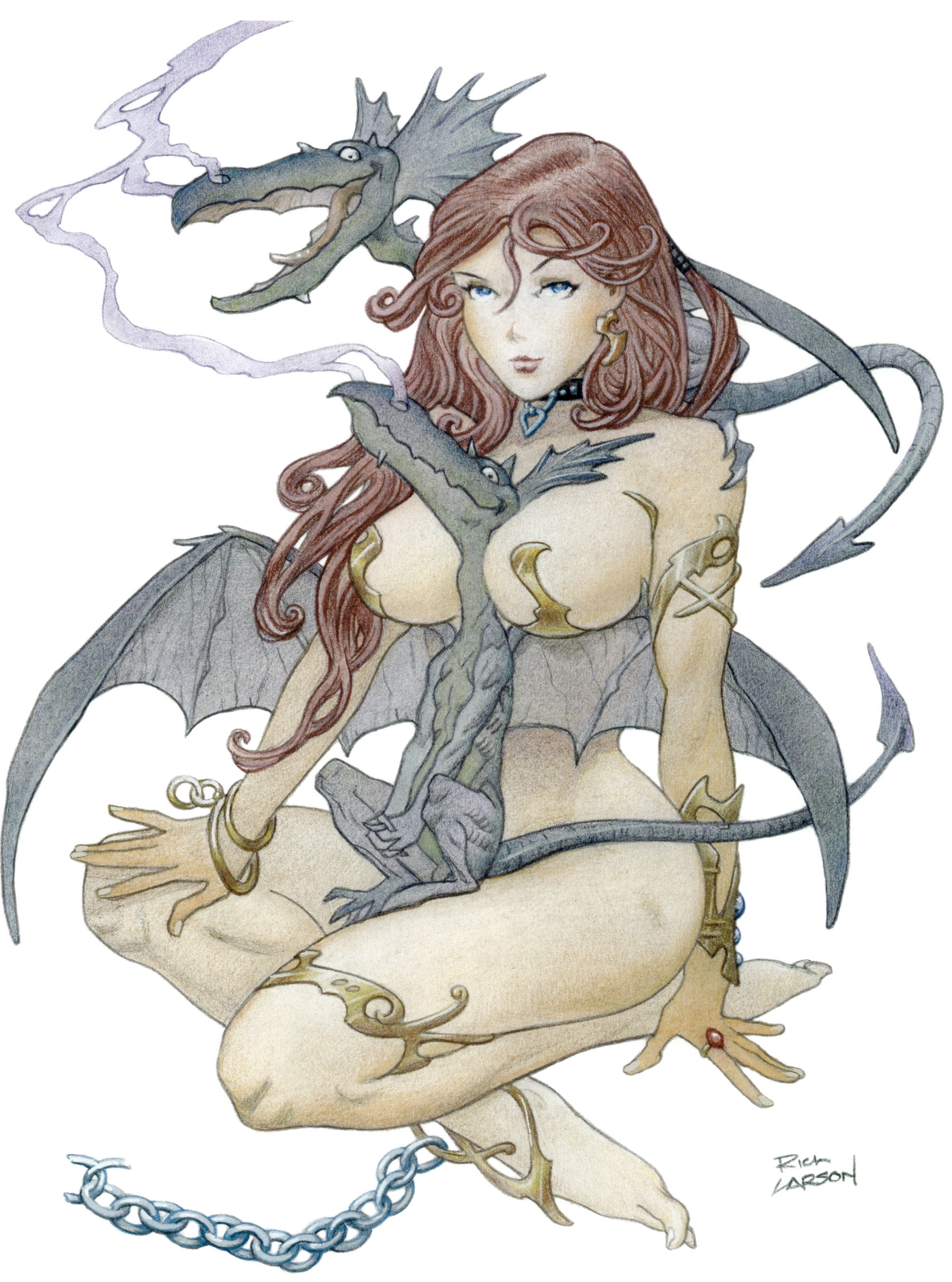

Rich Larson

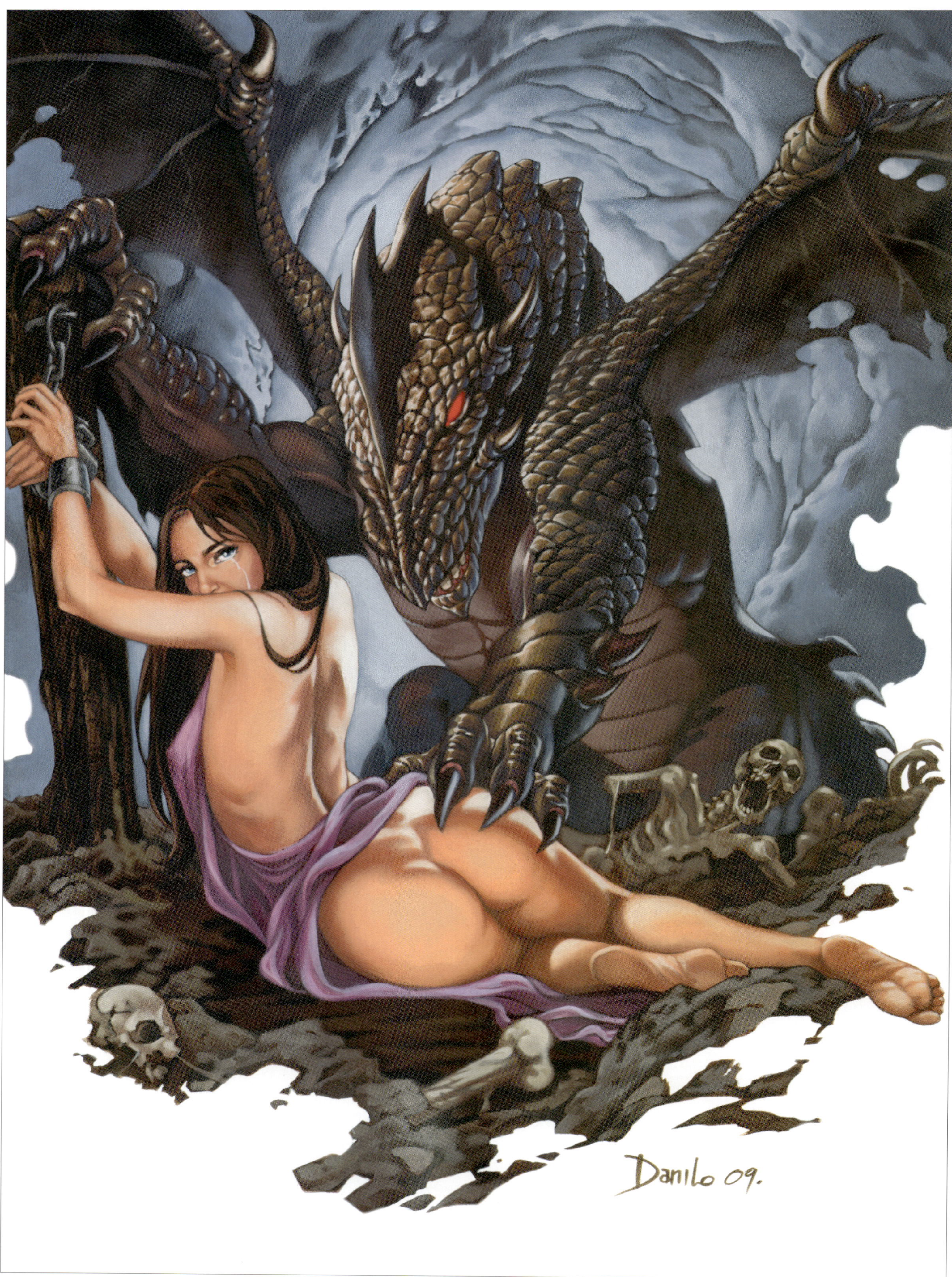

Danilo Guida

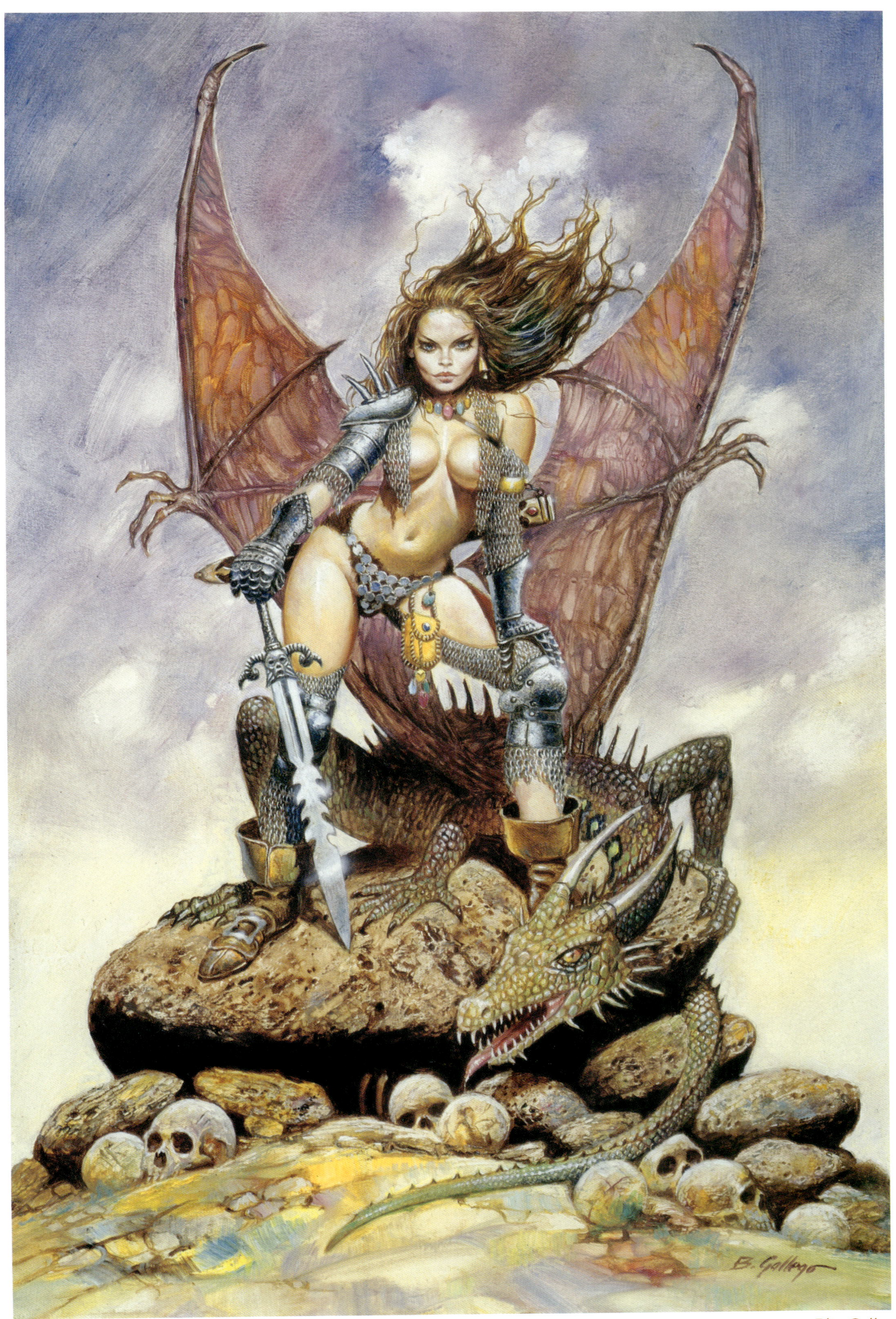

Blas Gallego

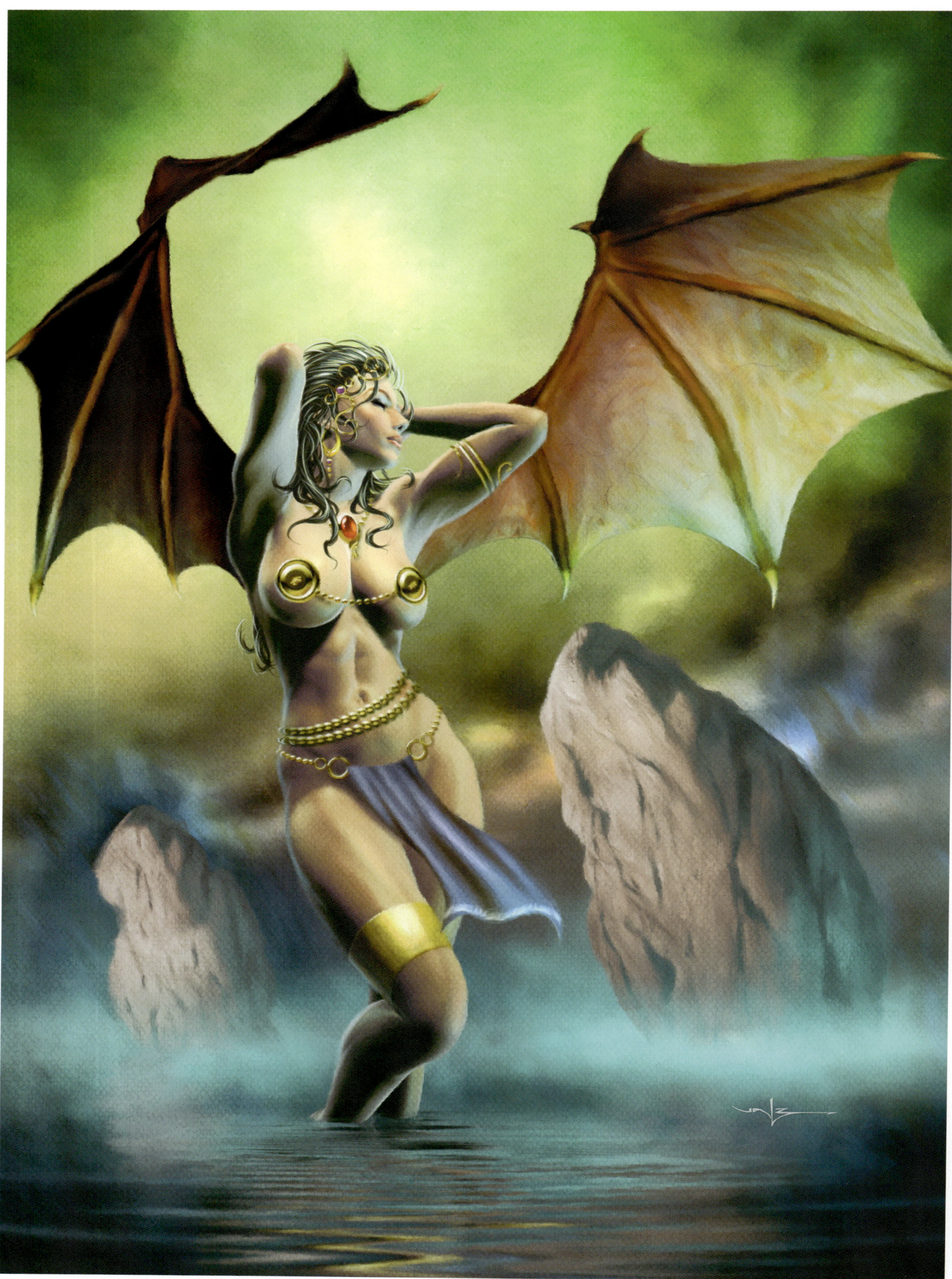

Carlos Valenzuela

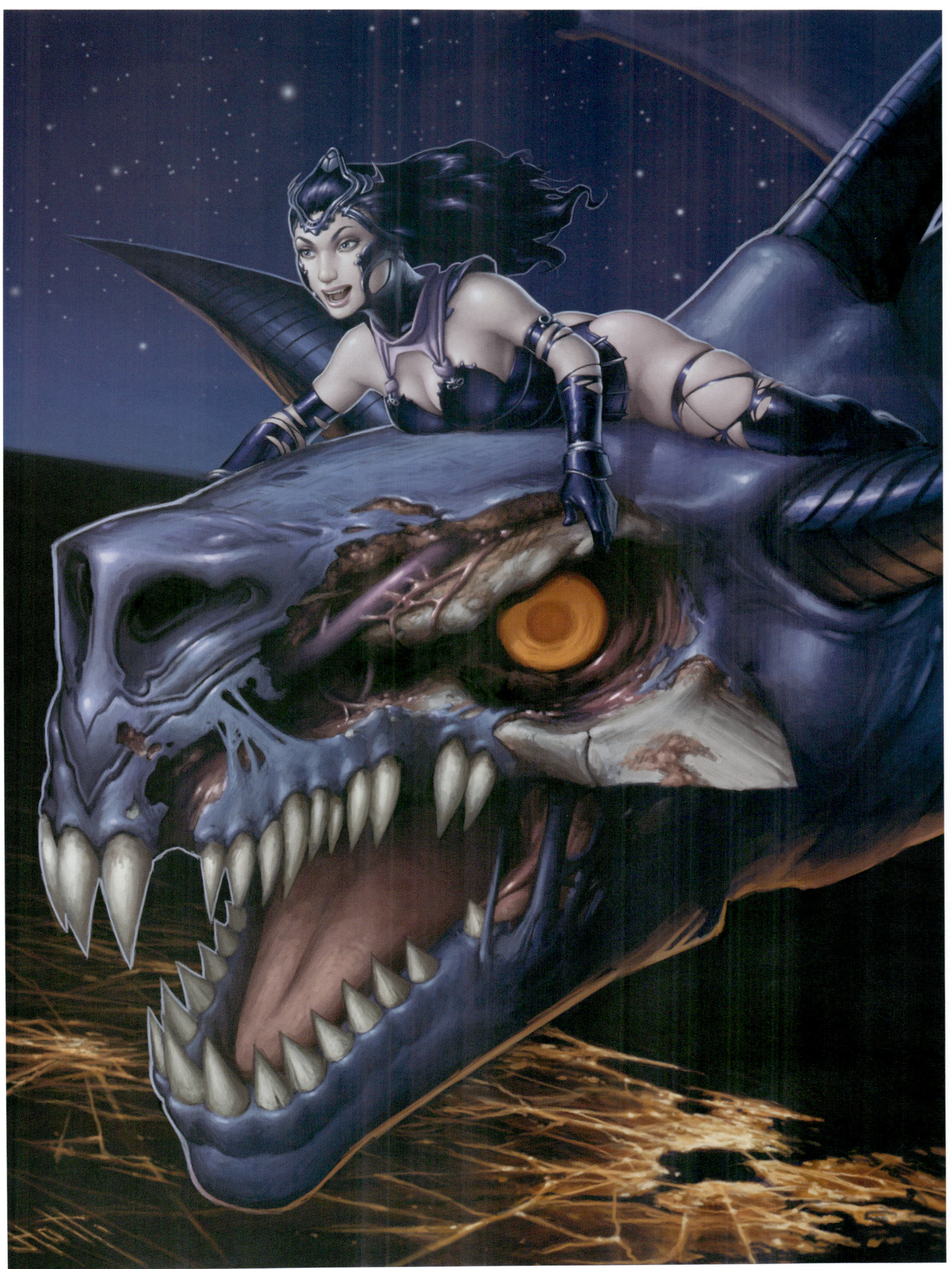

James Hottinger

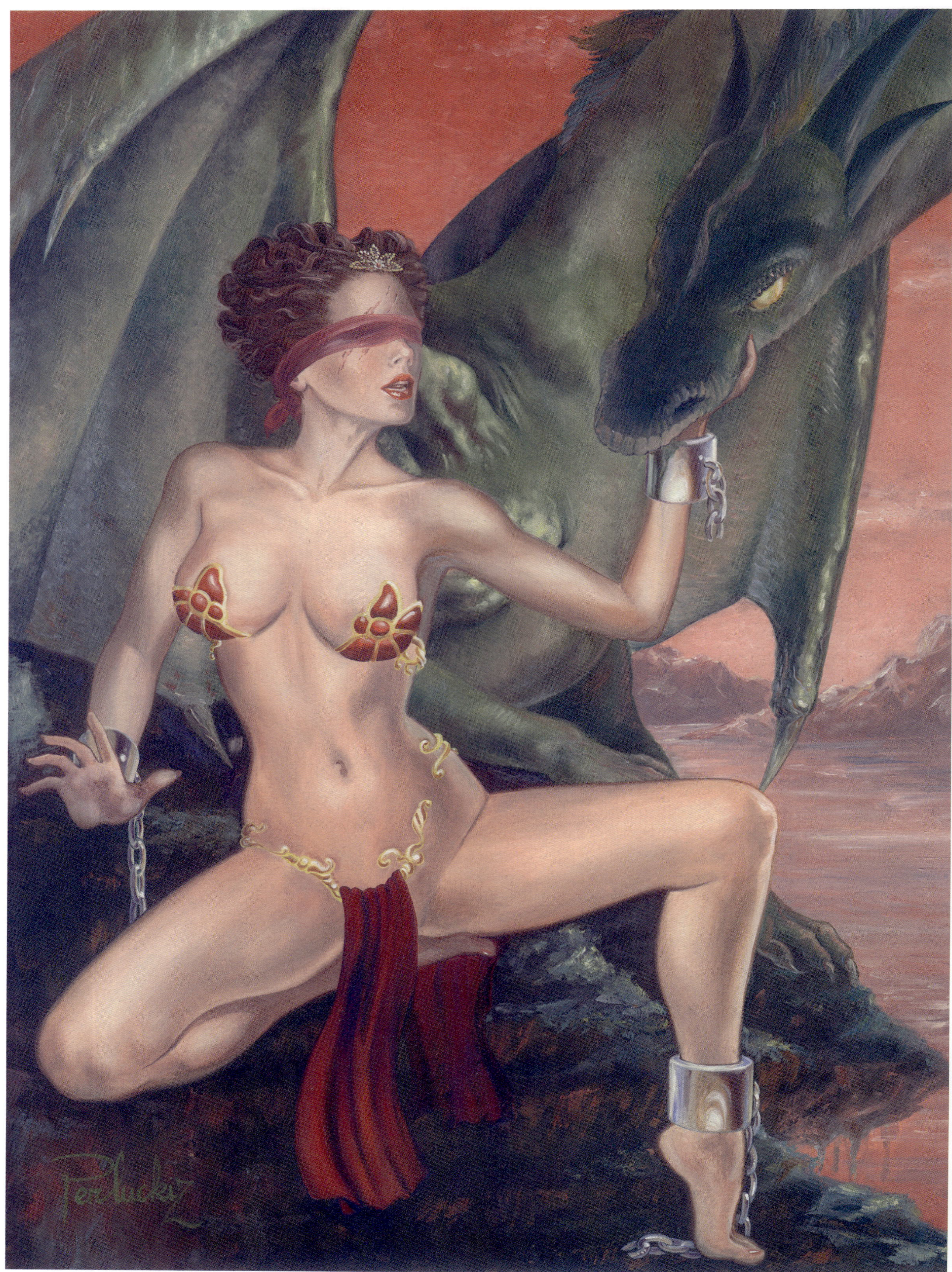

Perla Pilucki

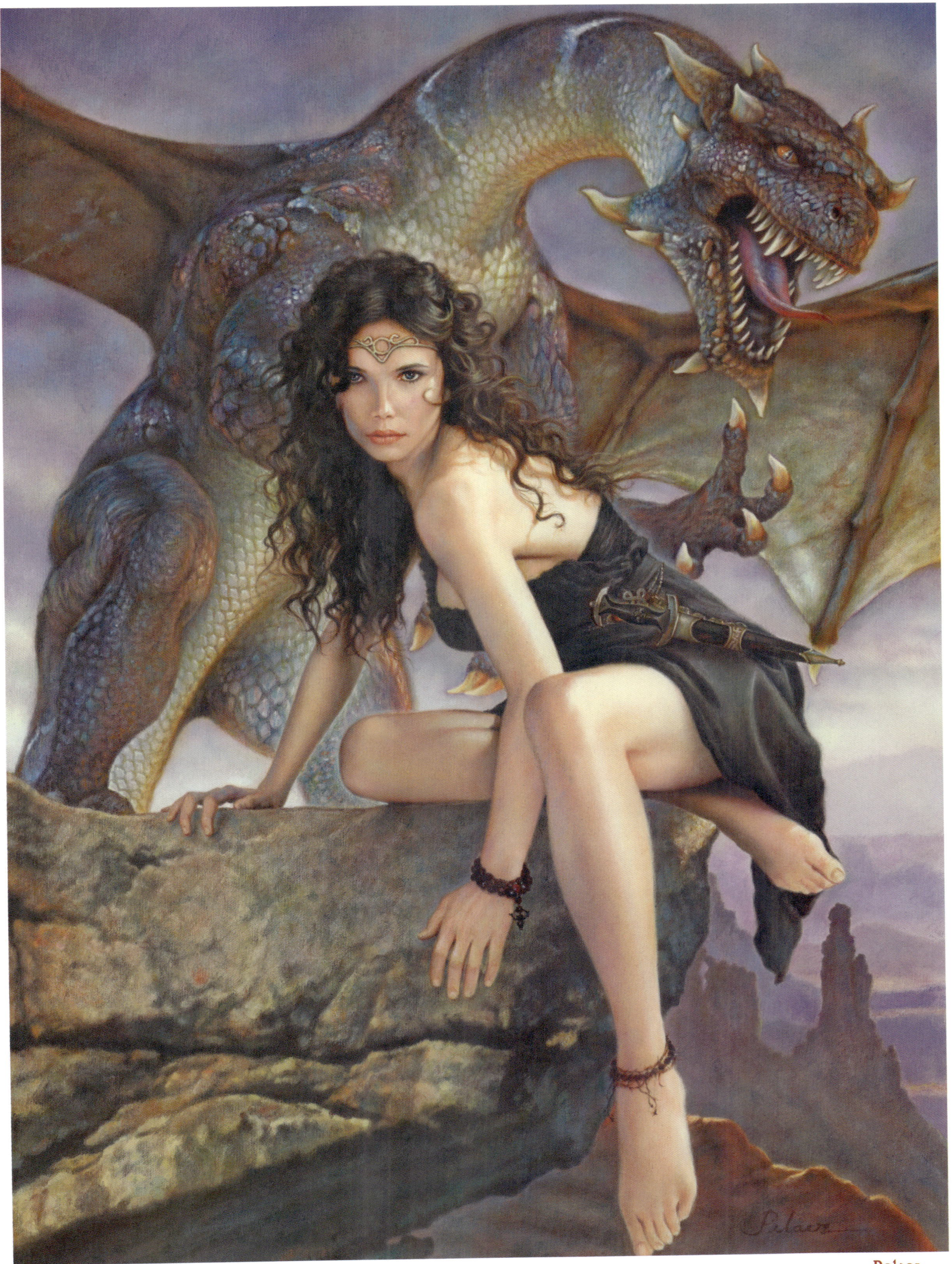

Pelaez

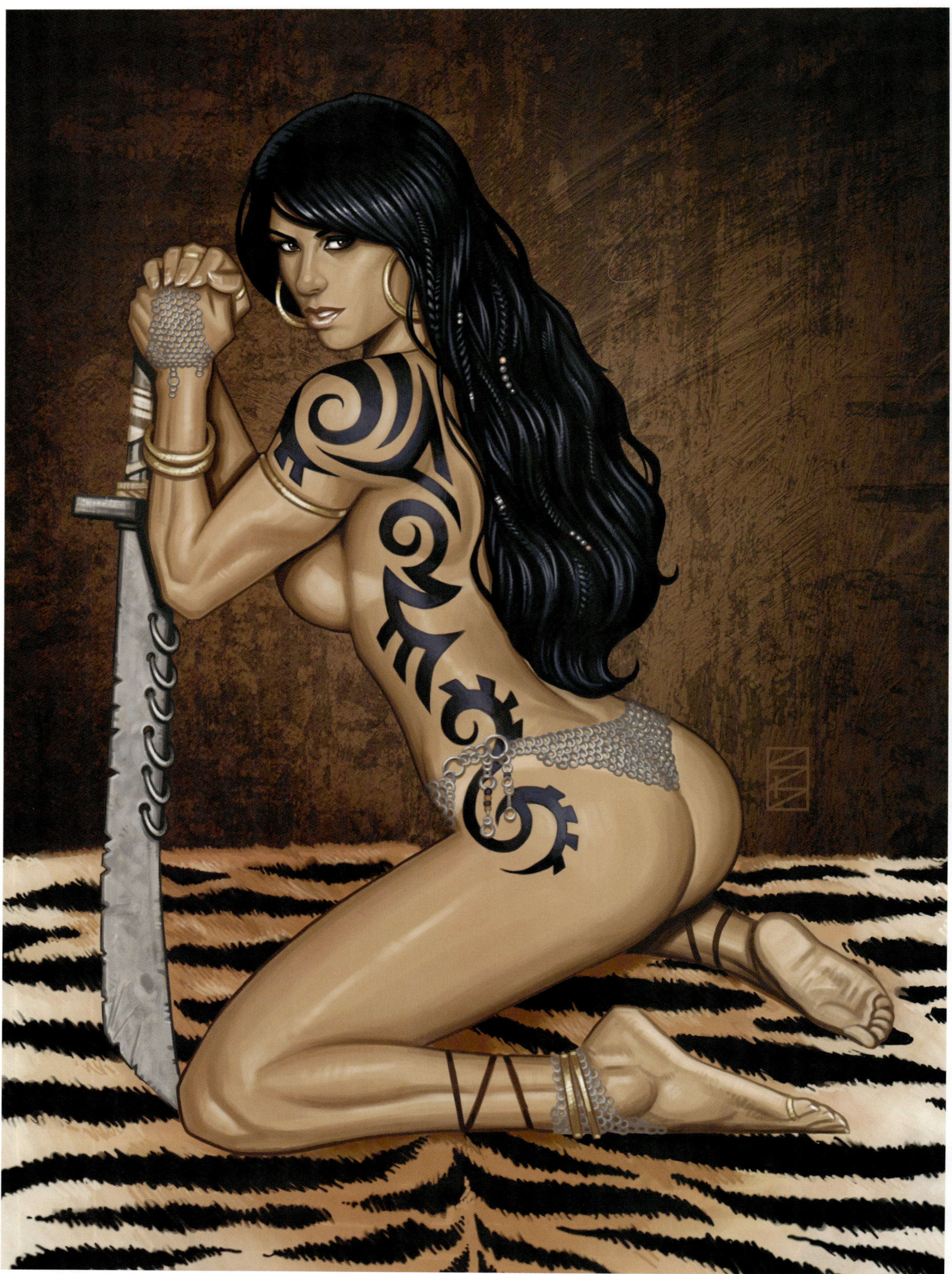

Scott Blair

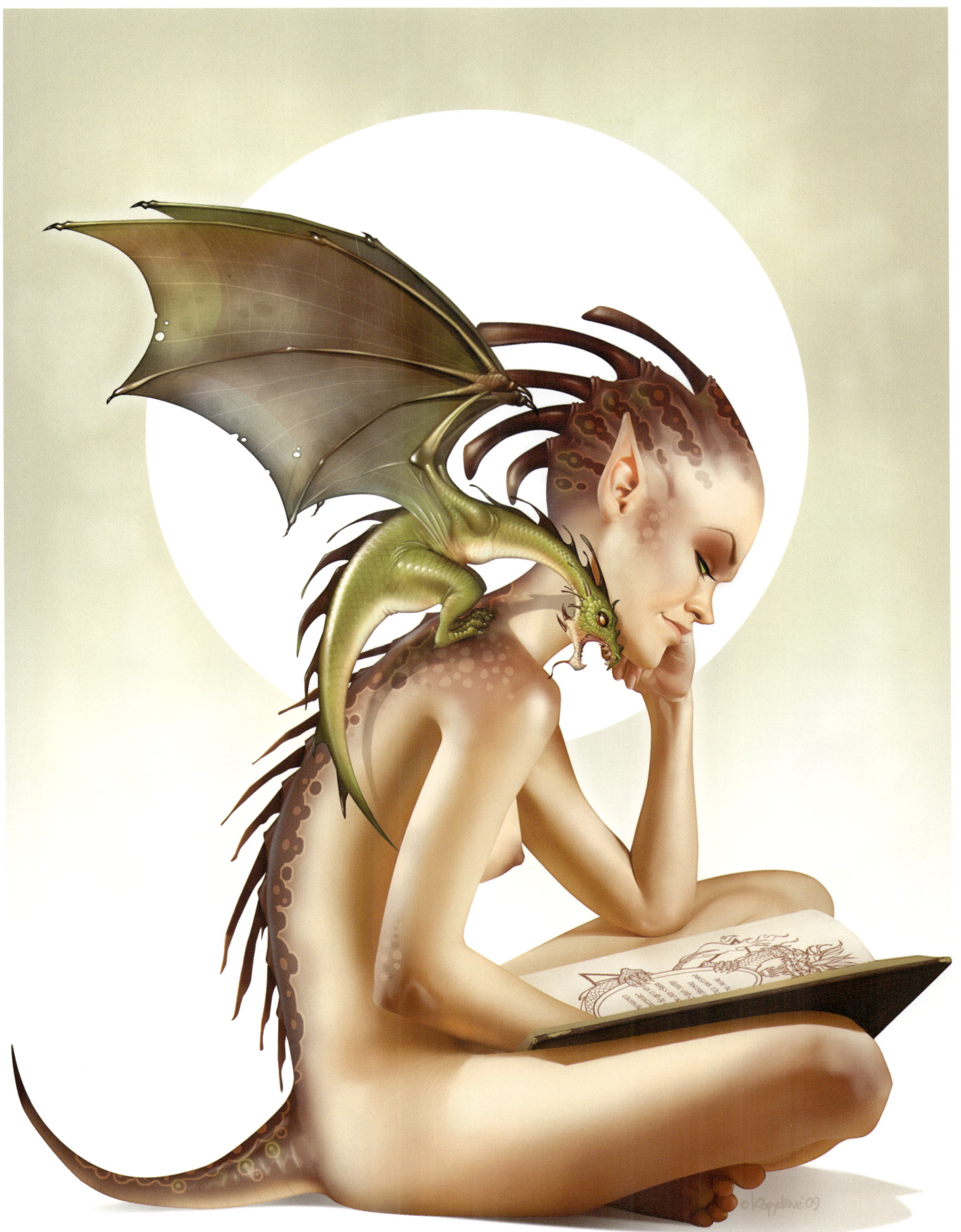

David Dunstan

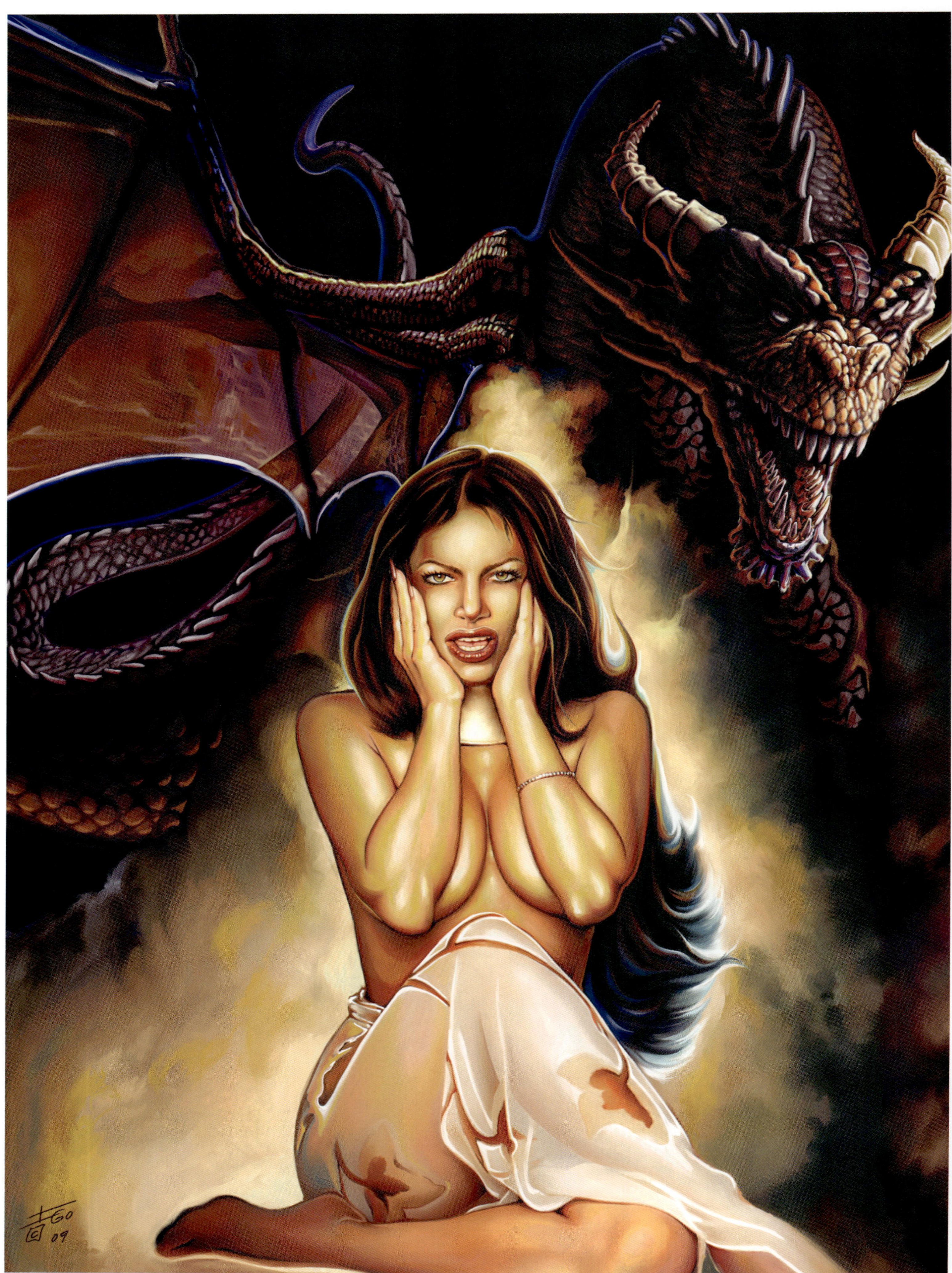

Inaki Ormaetxea

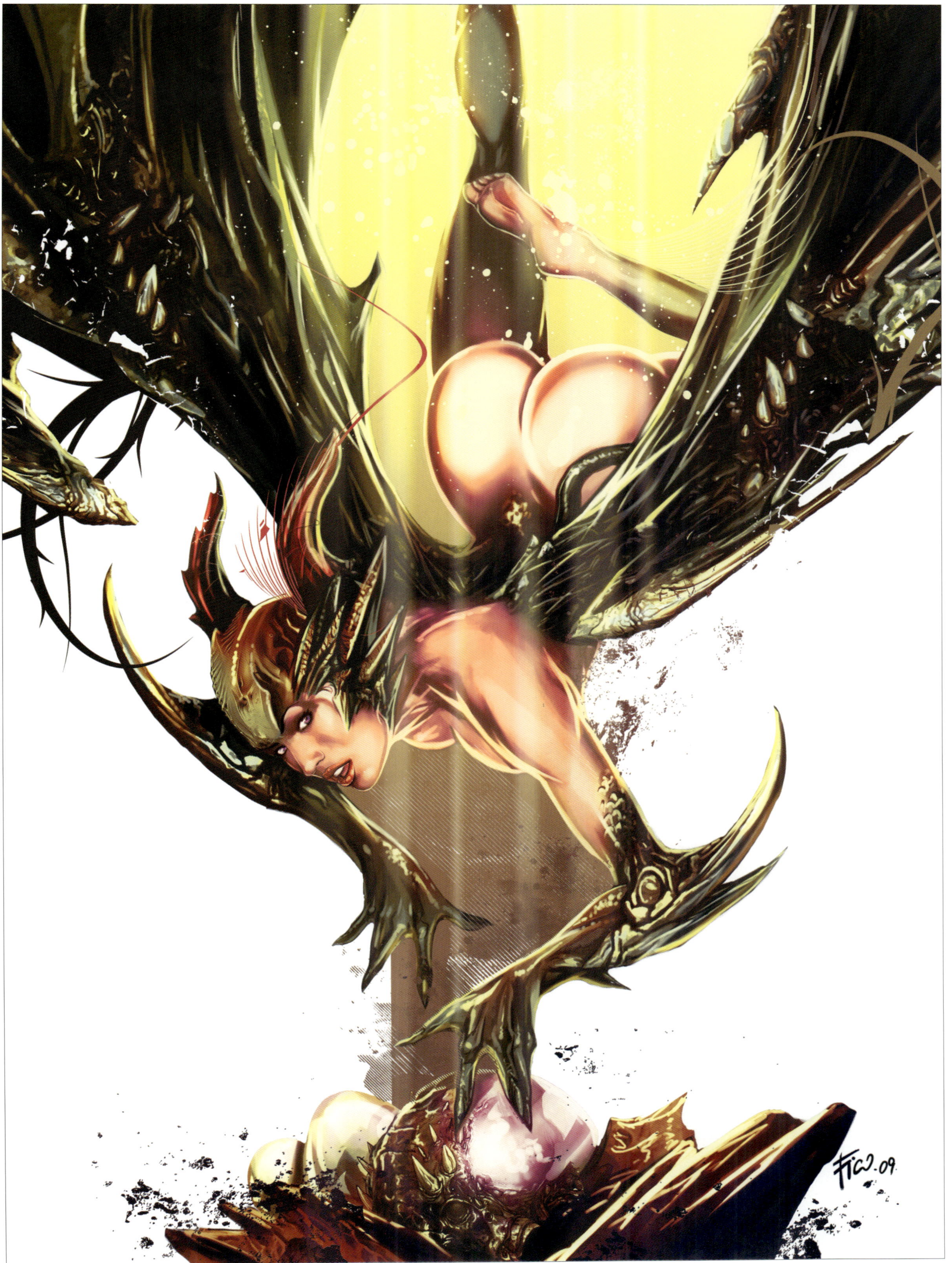

Federico Ossio

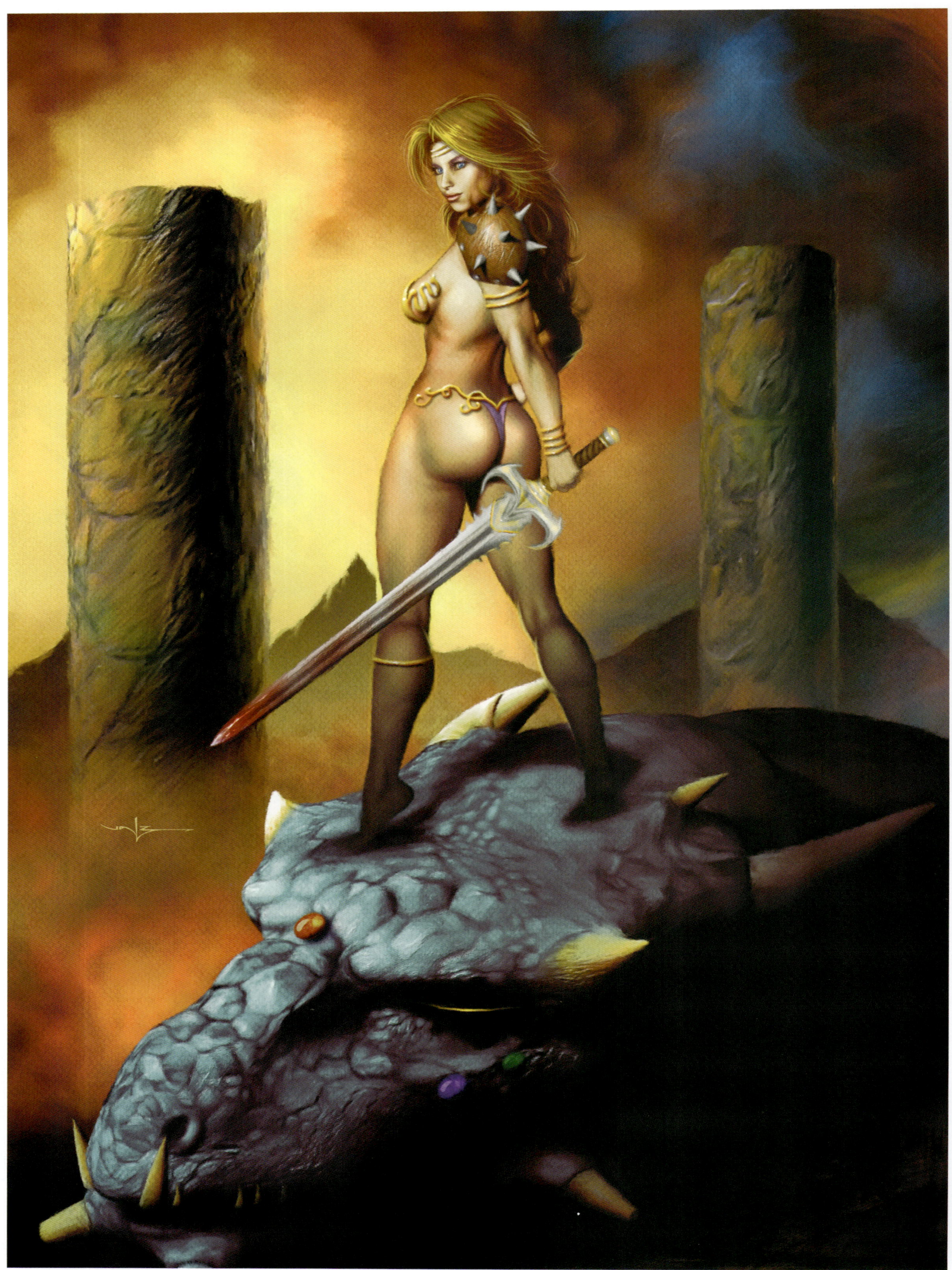

Carlos Valenzuela

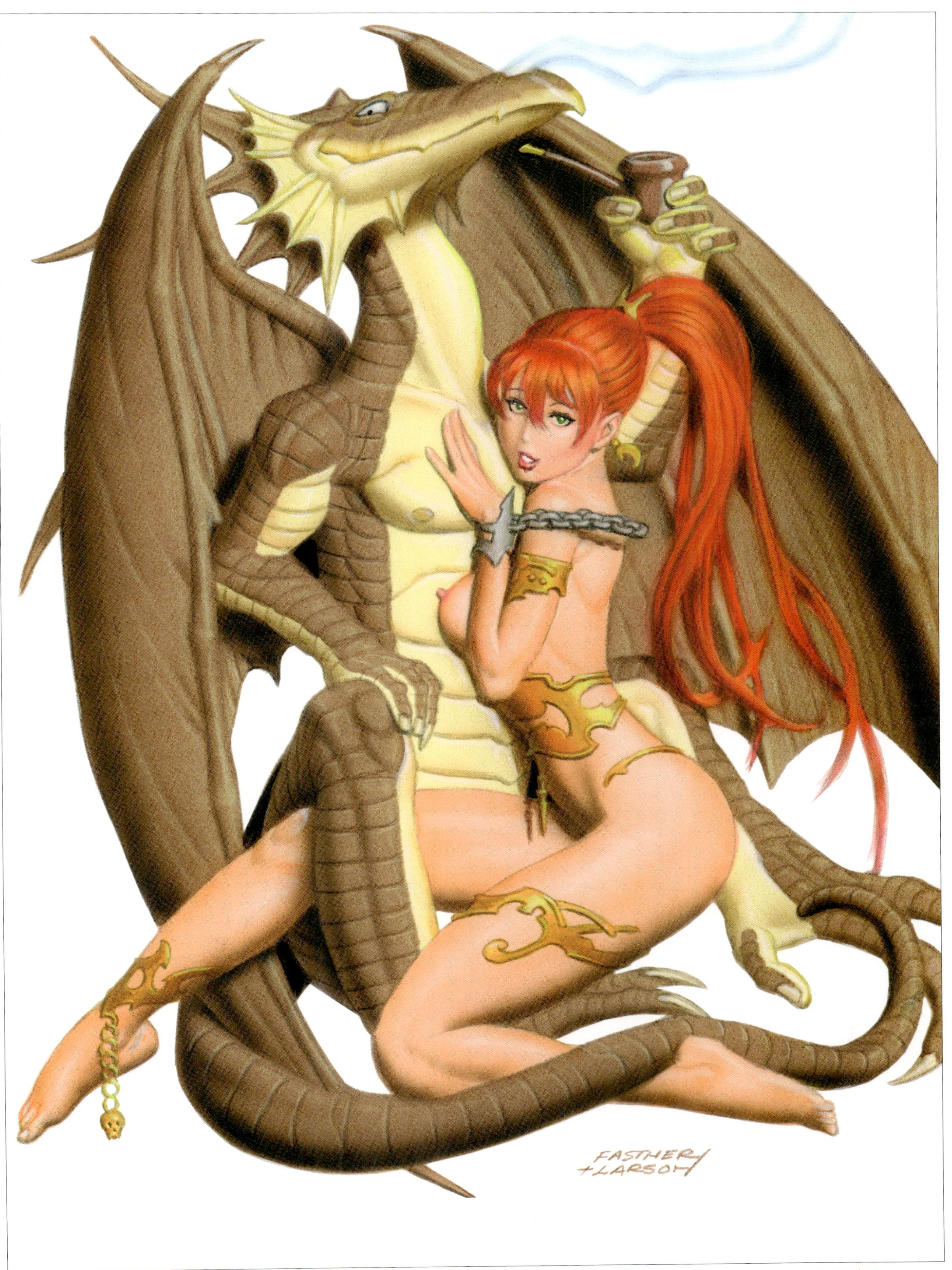

Steve Fastner & Rich Larson

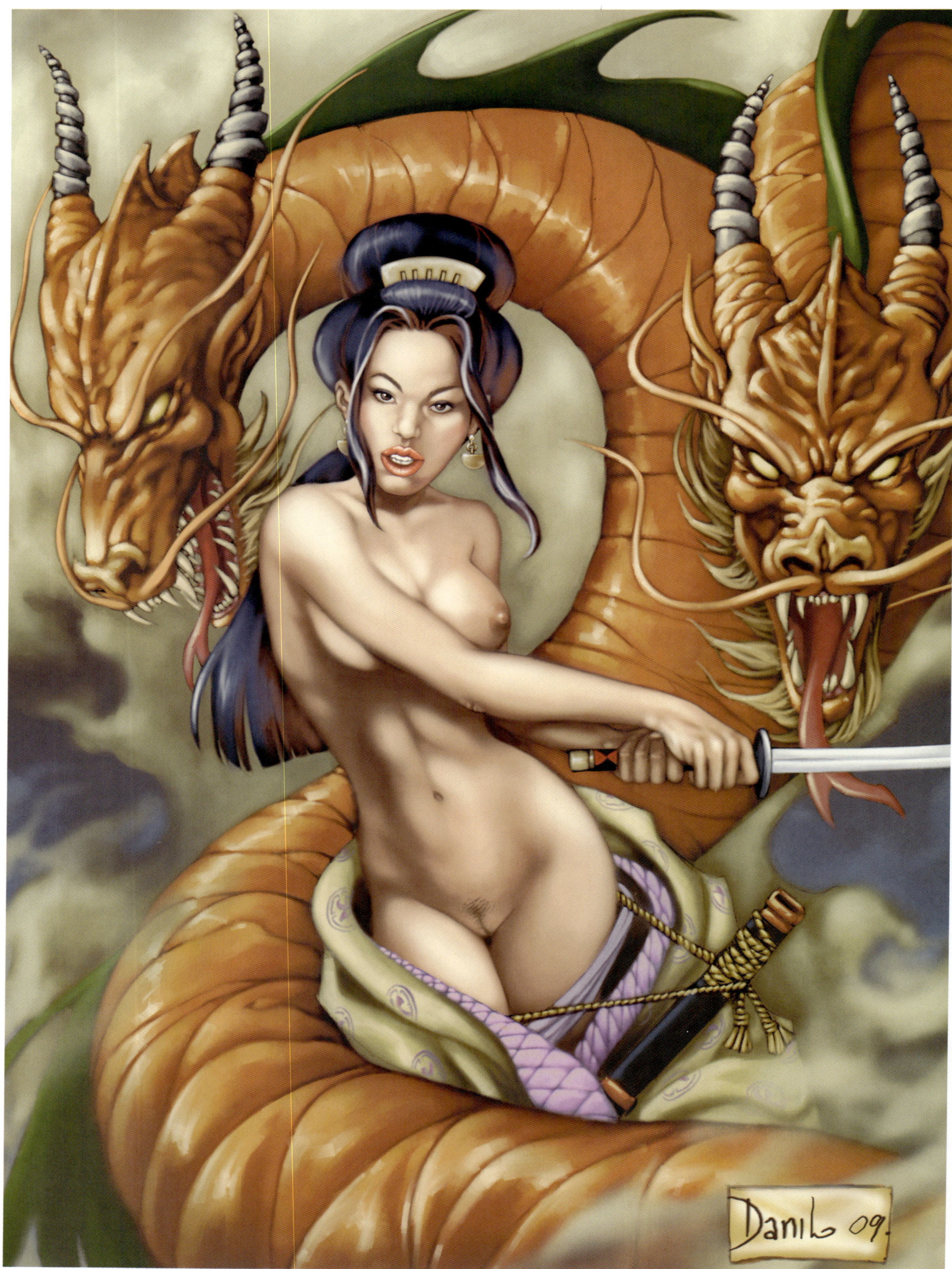

Danilo Guida

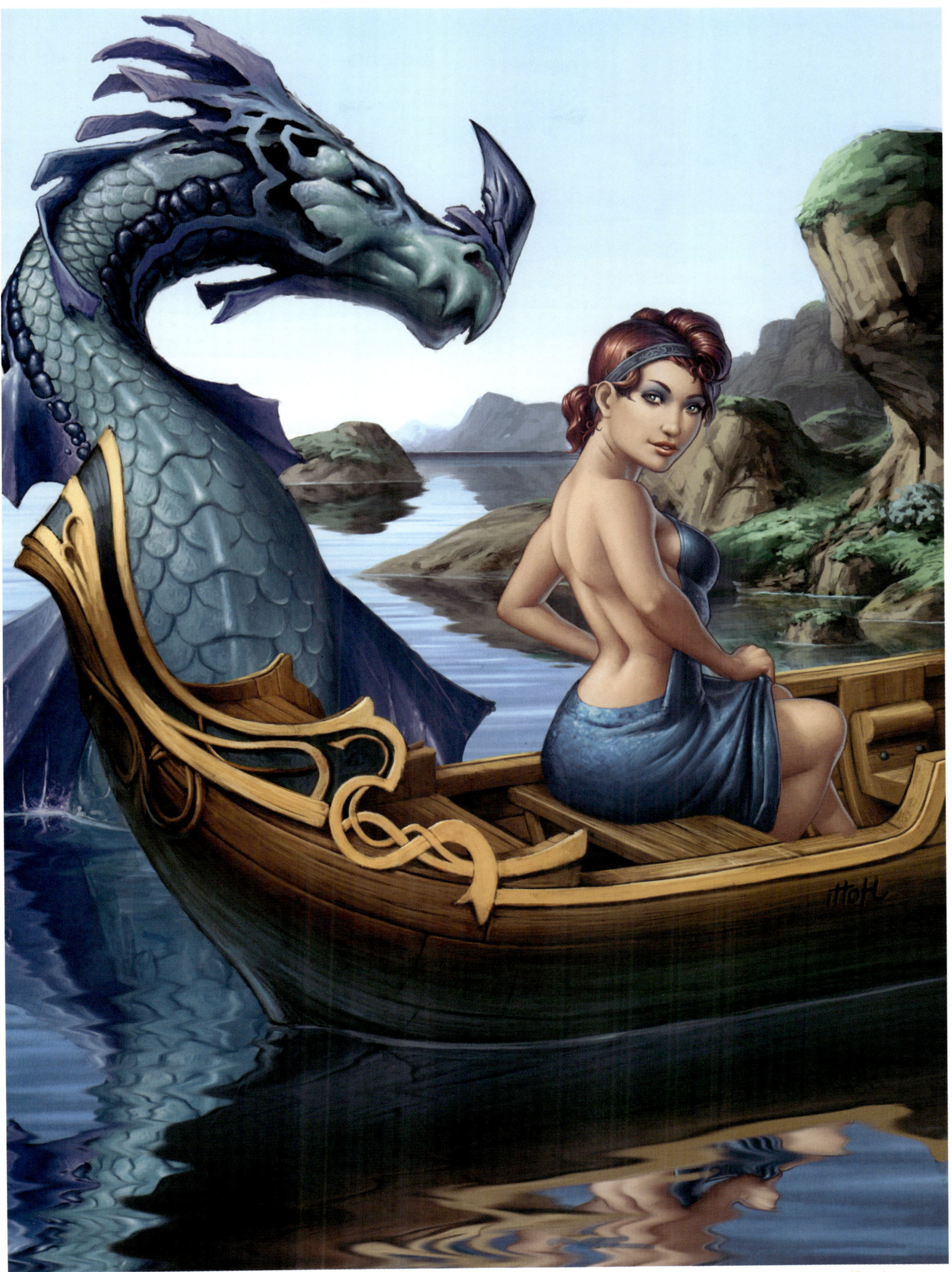

James Hottinger

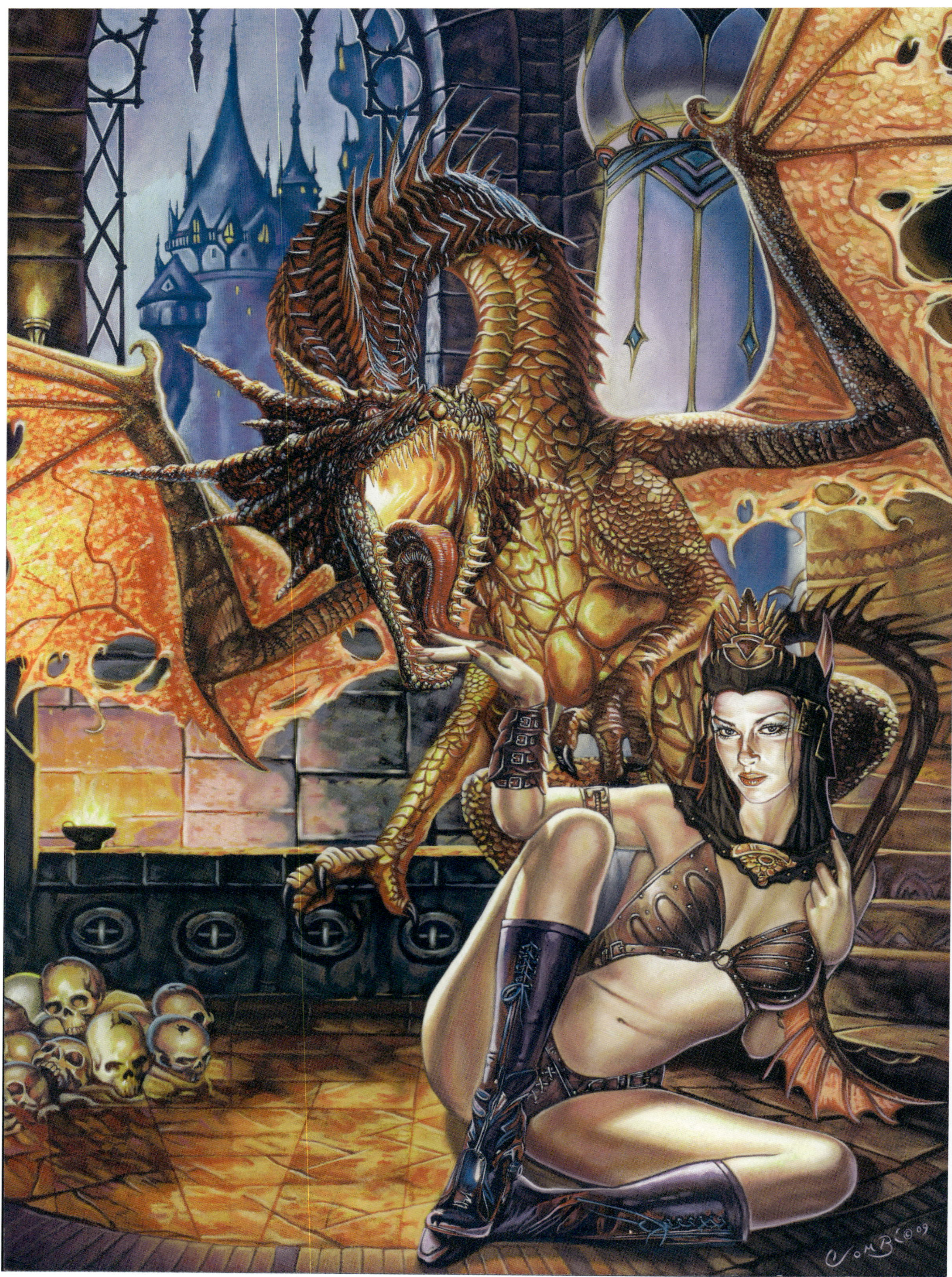

Federico Combi

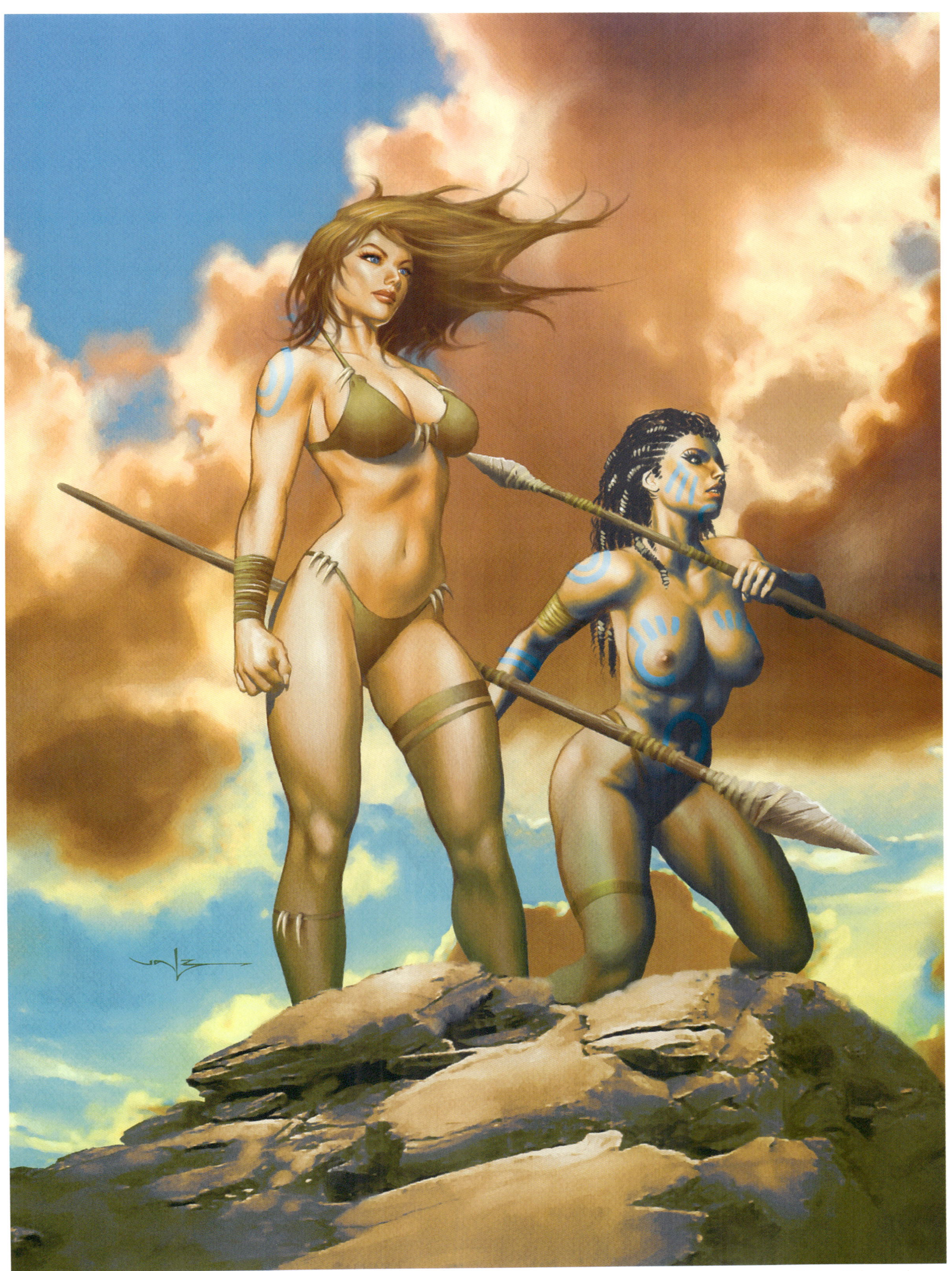

Carlos Valenzuela

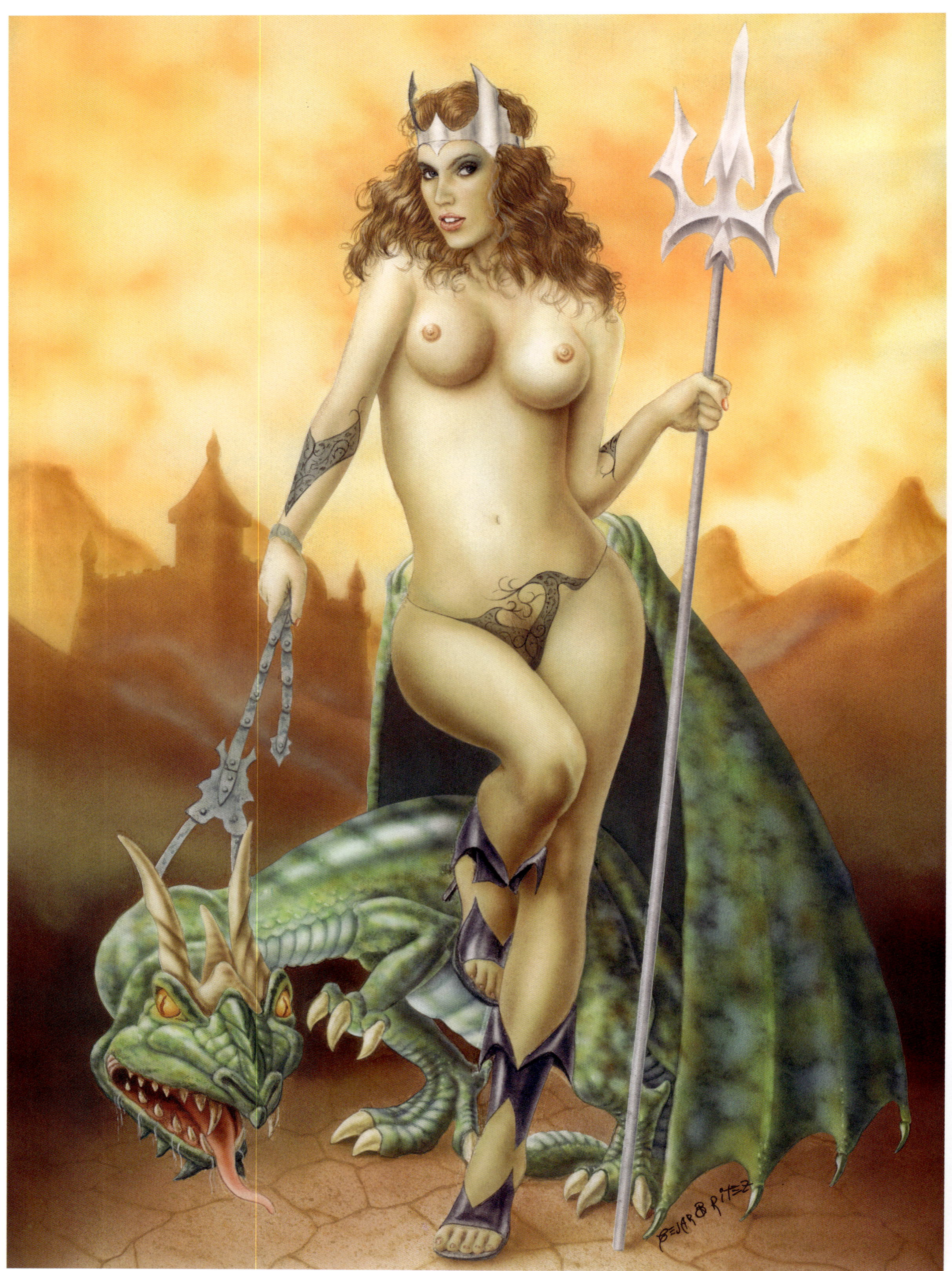

Cesar Britez

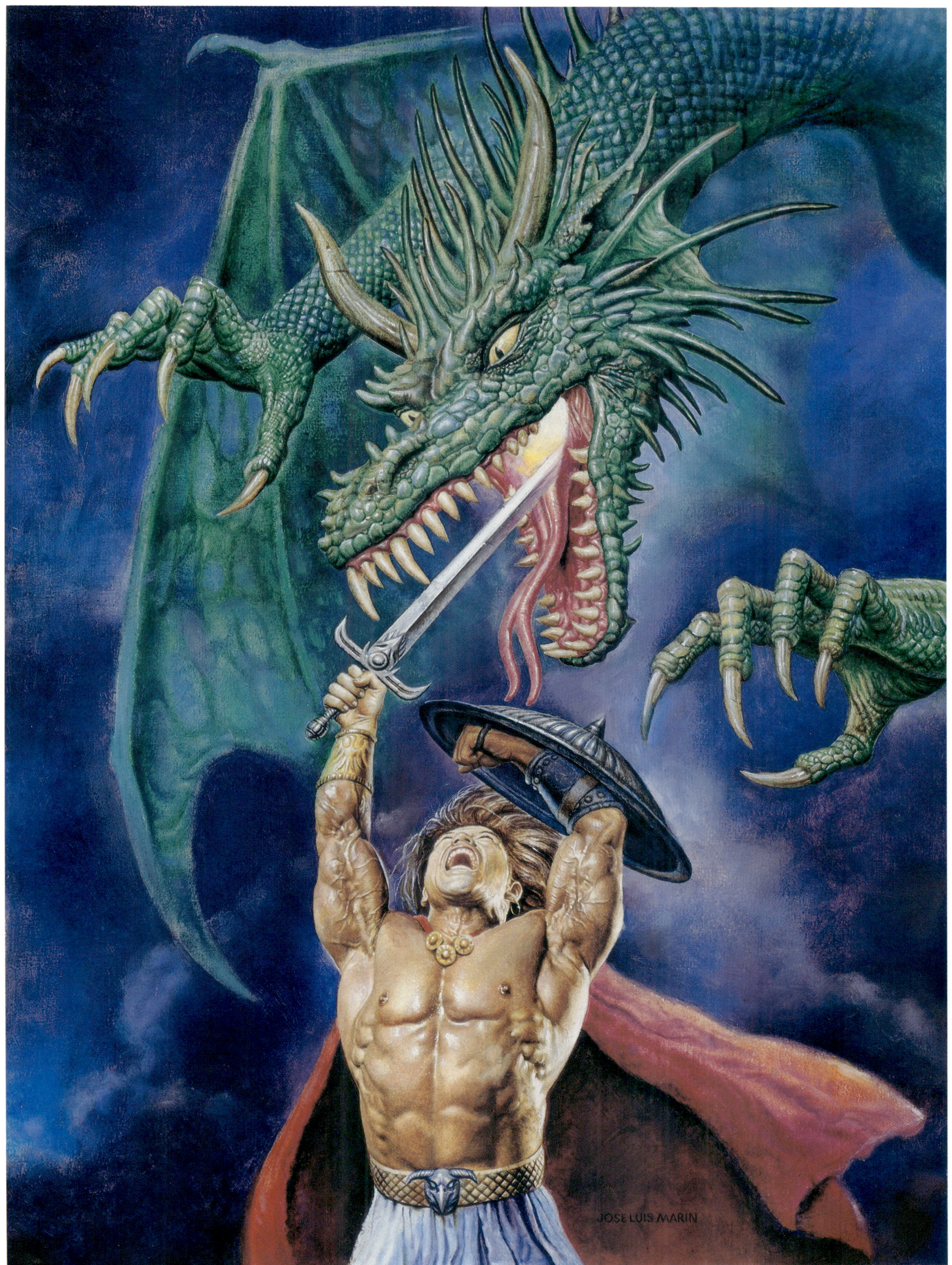

J.L. Marin

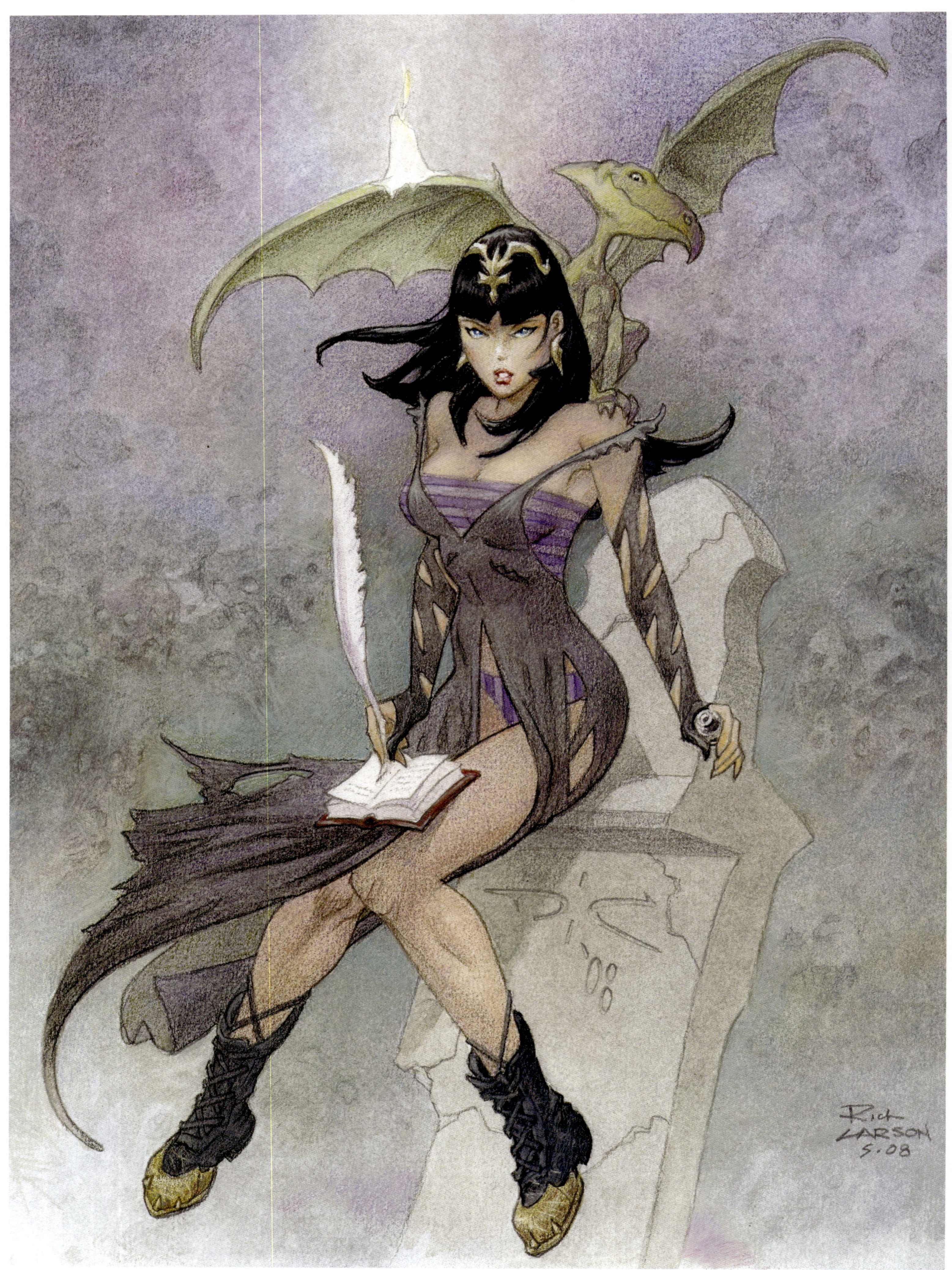

Rich Larson

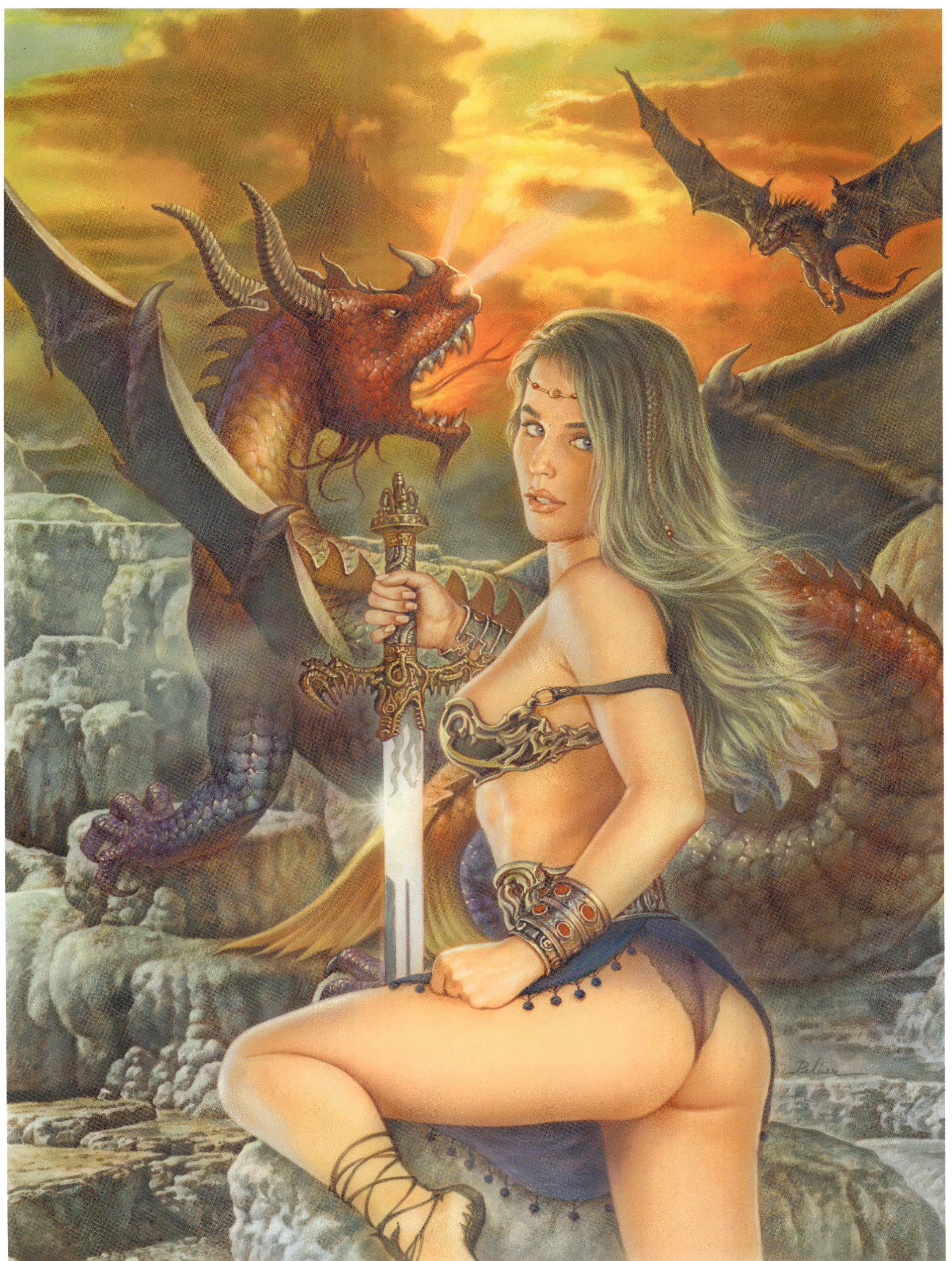

Pelaez

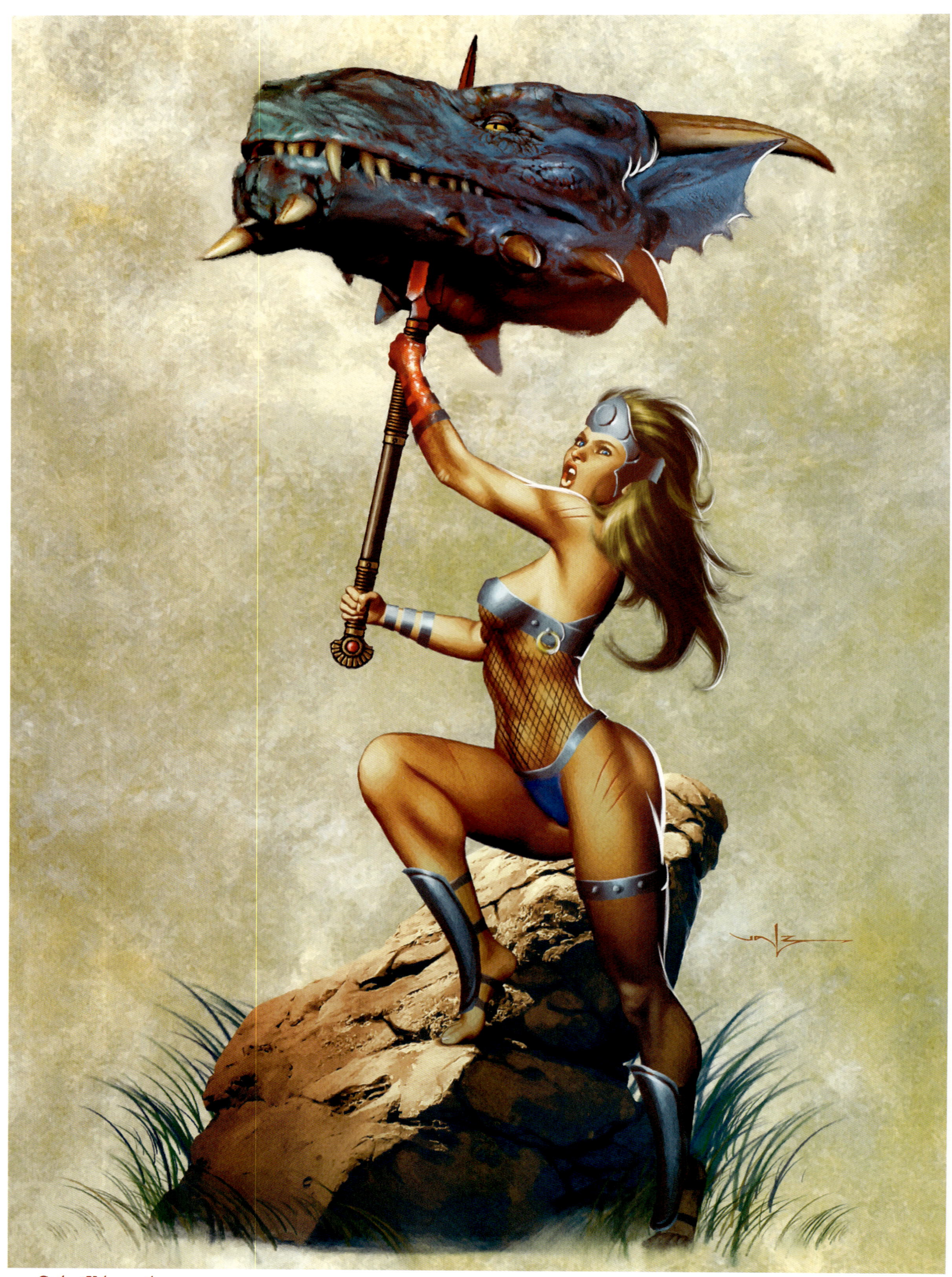

Carlos Valenzuela

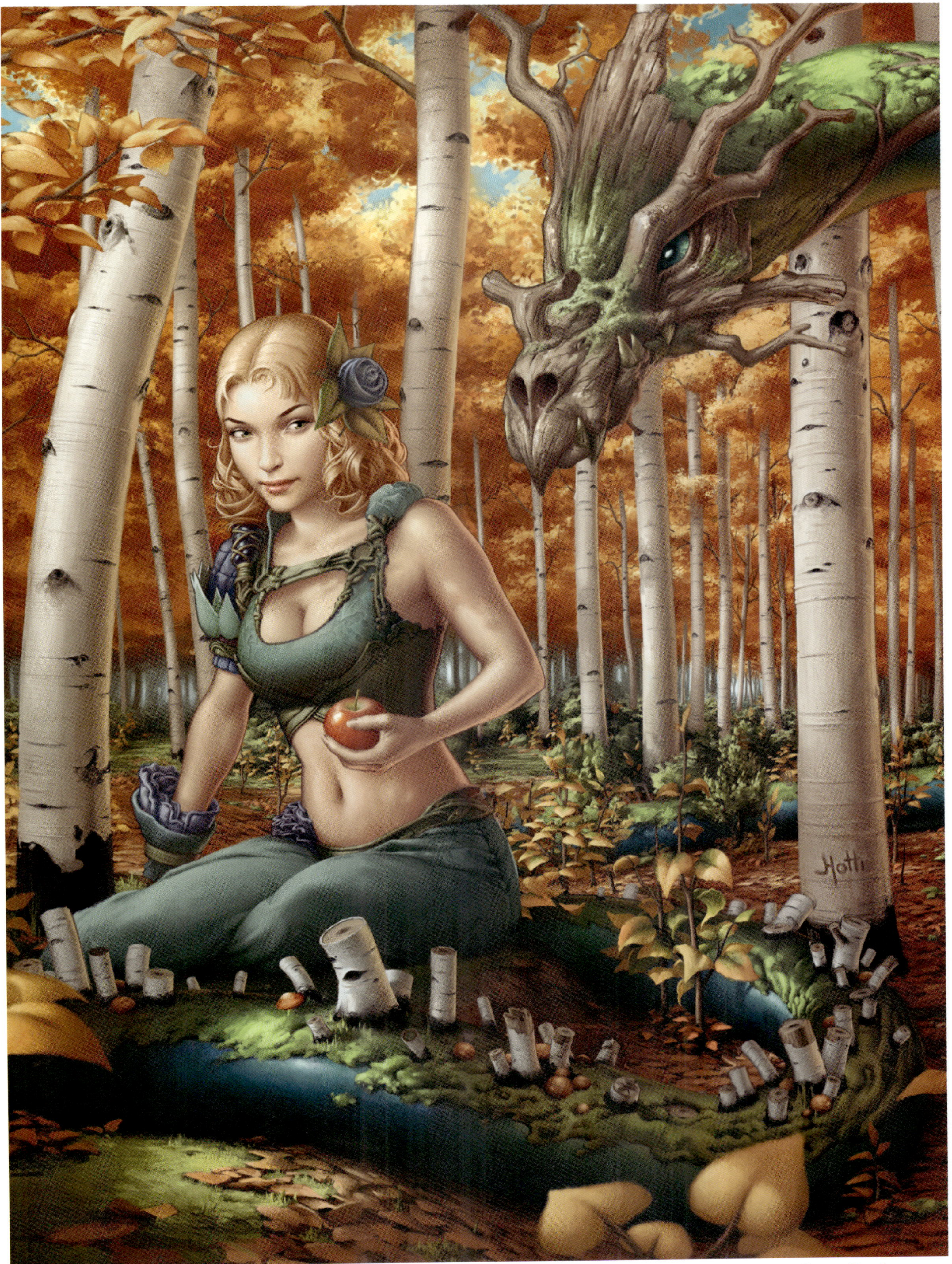

James Hottinger

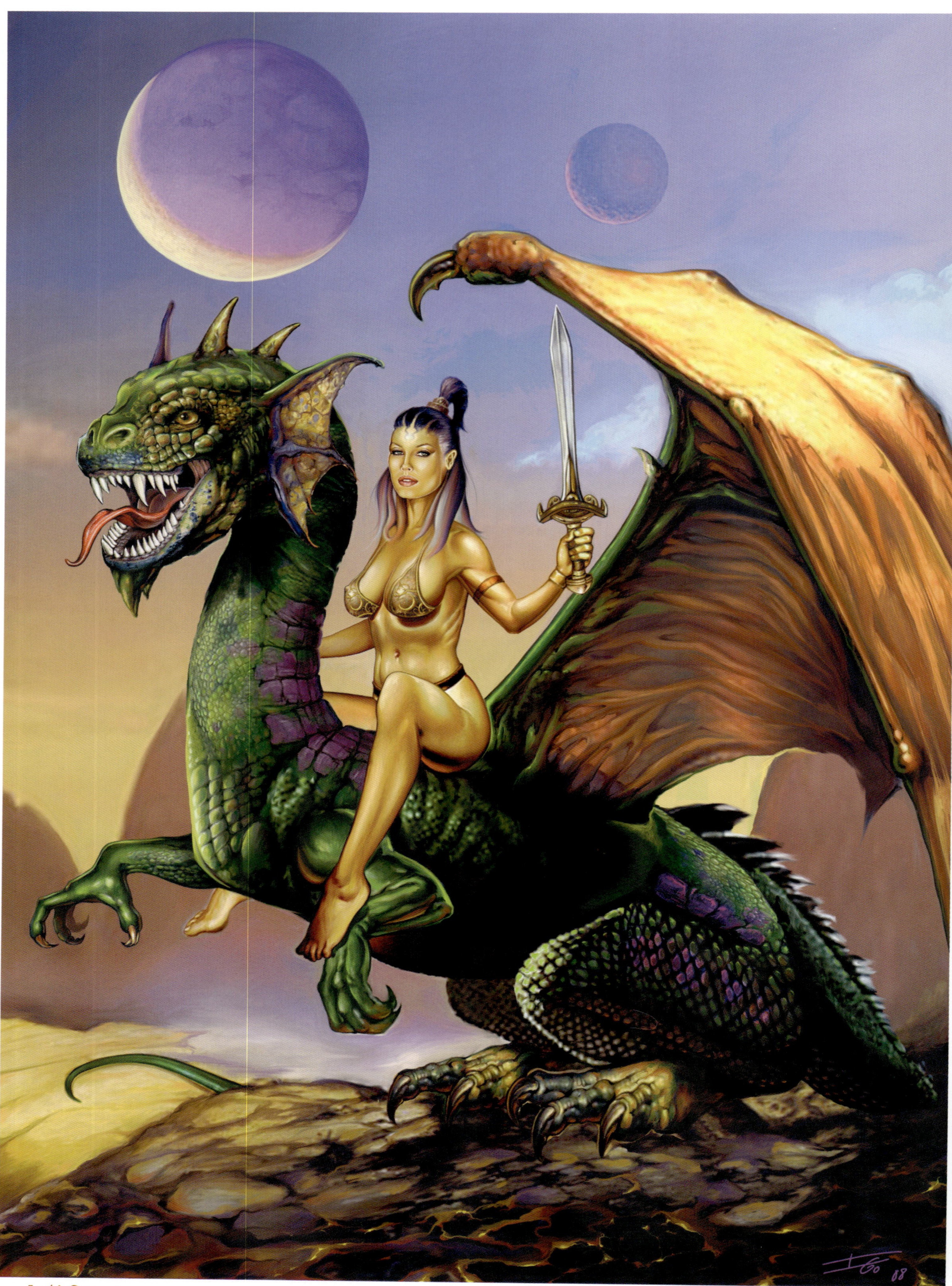

Inaki Ormaetxea

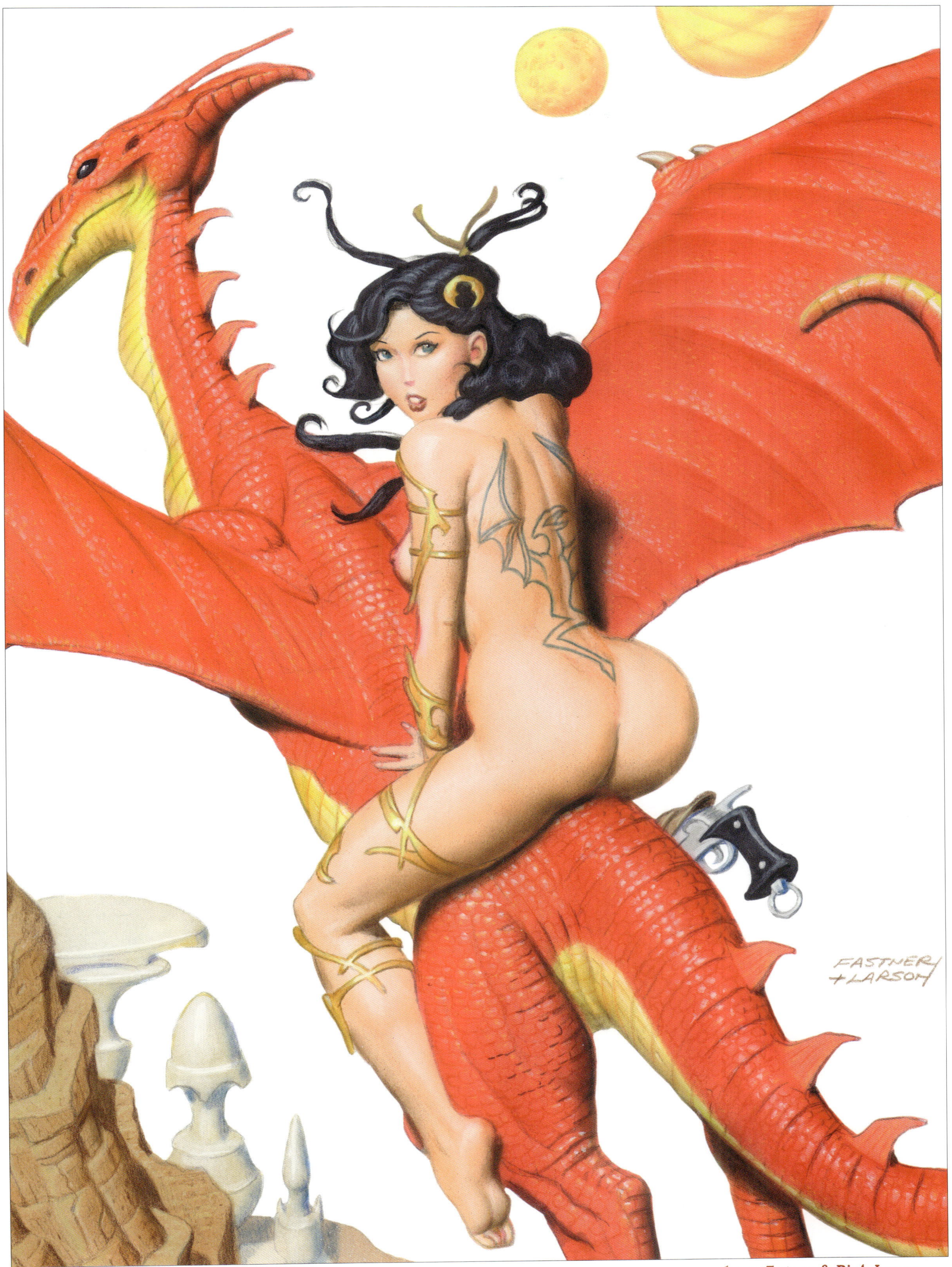

Steve Fastner & Rich Larson

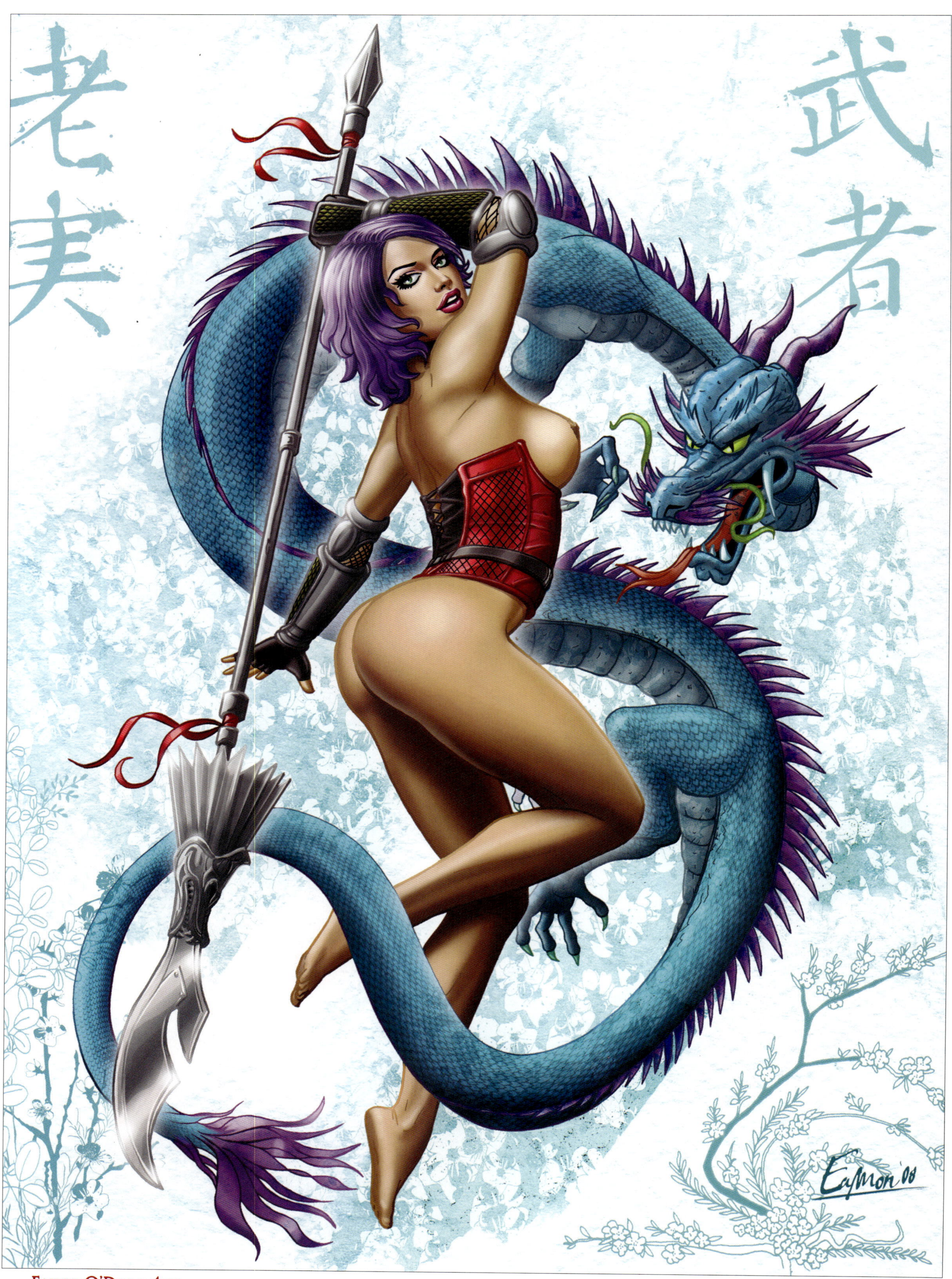

Eamon O'Donoghue

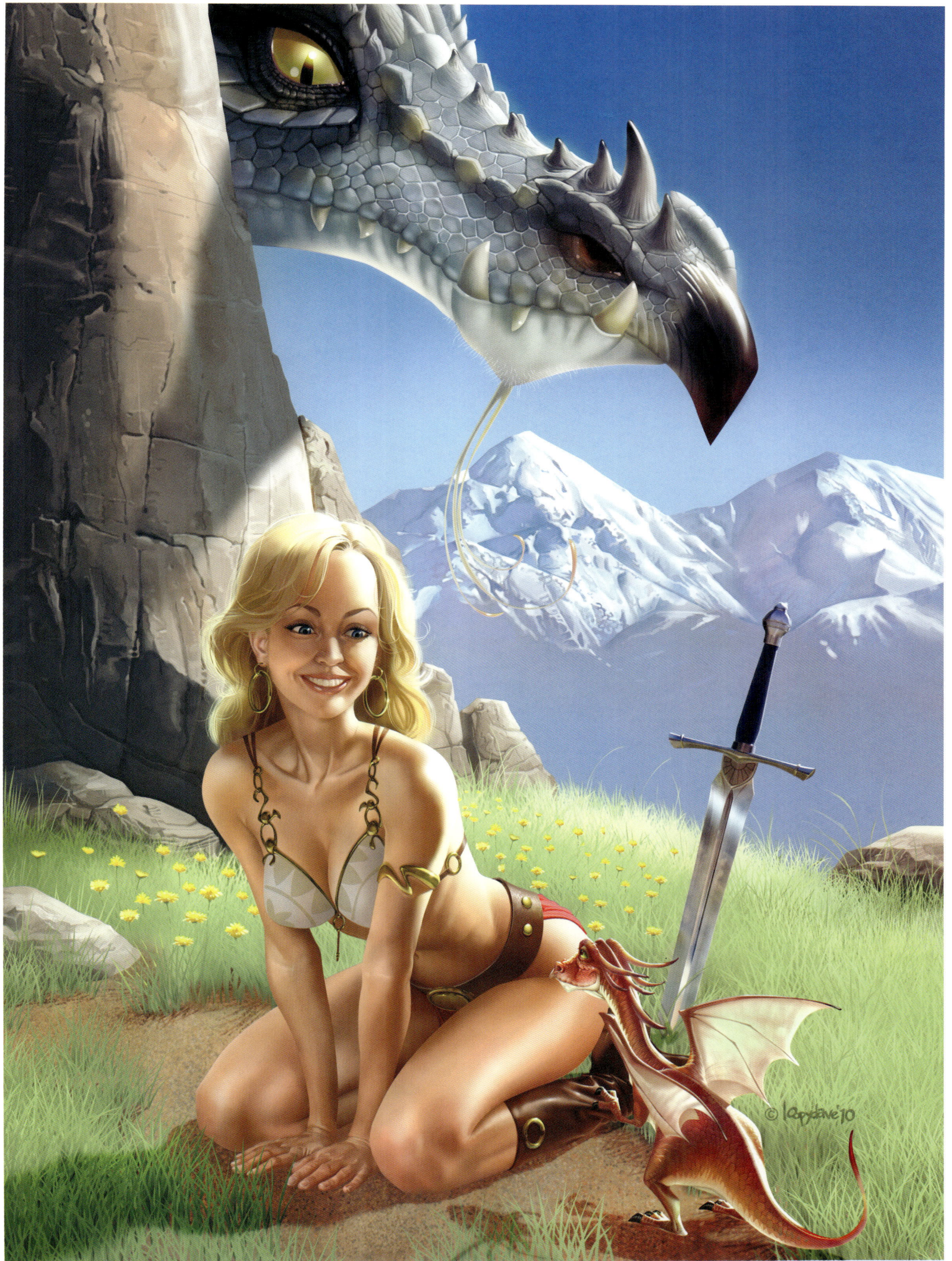

David Dunstan

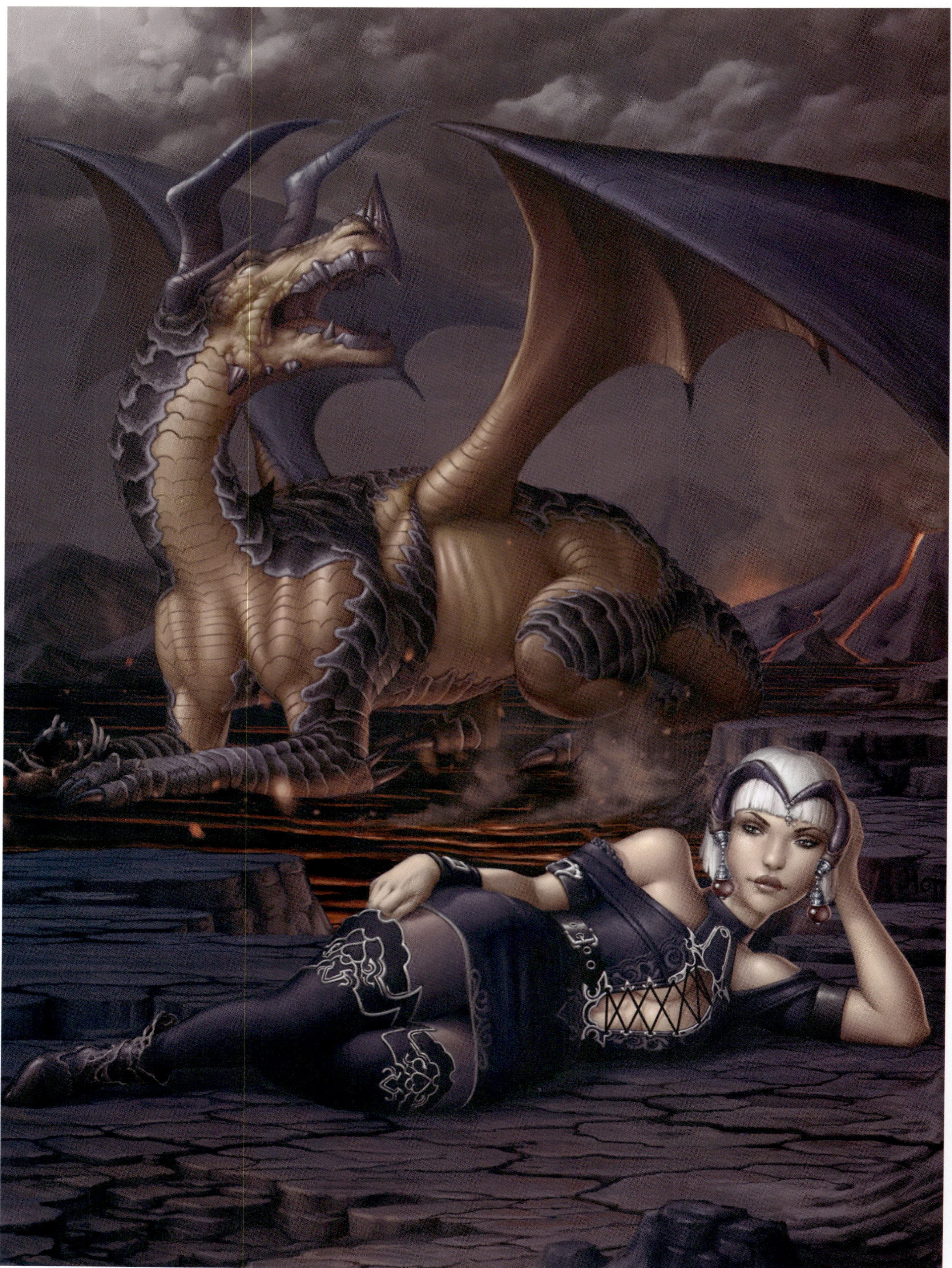

James Hottinger

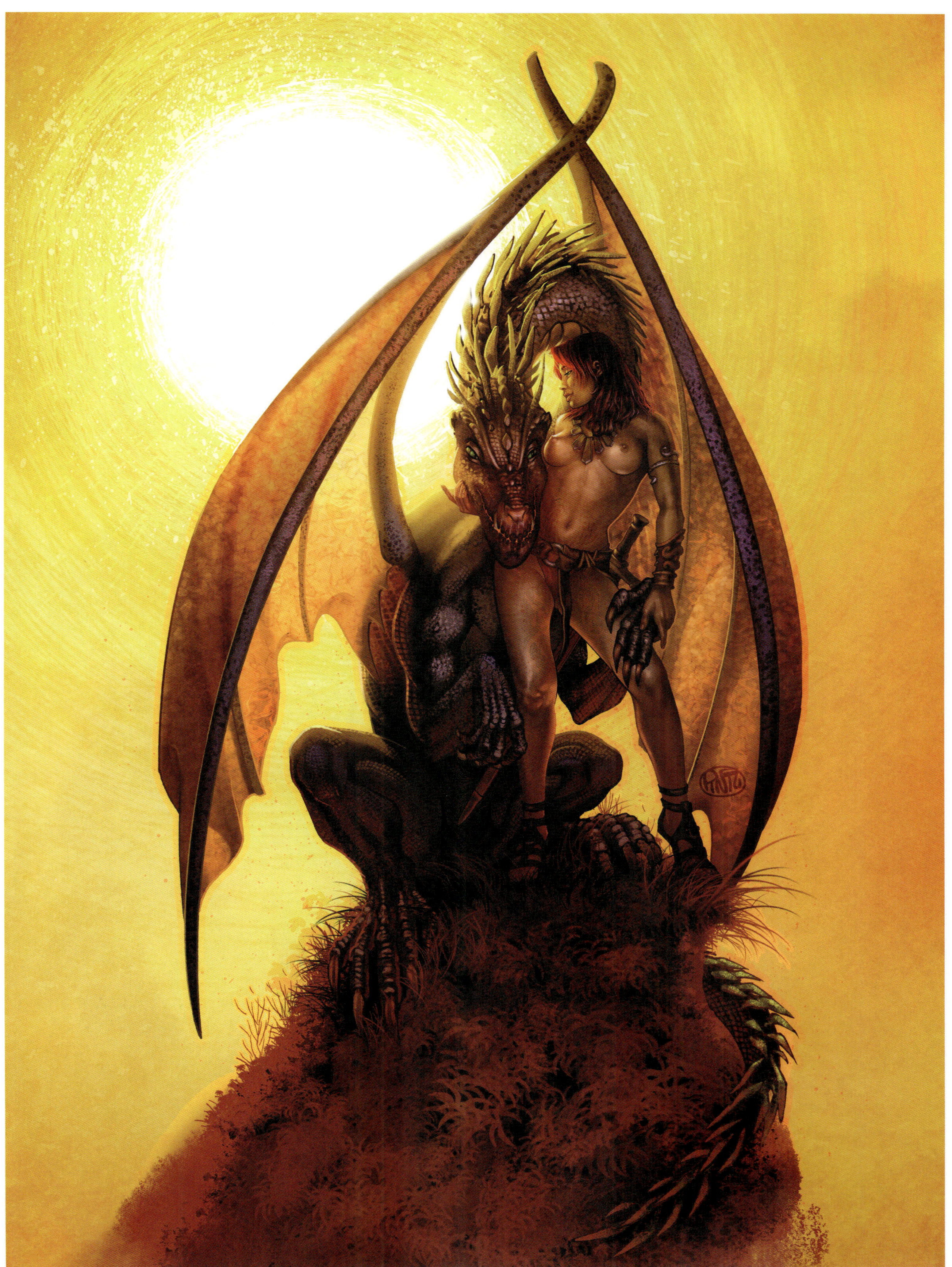

Pintuday

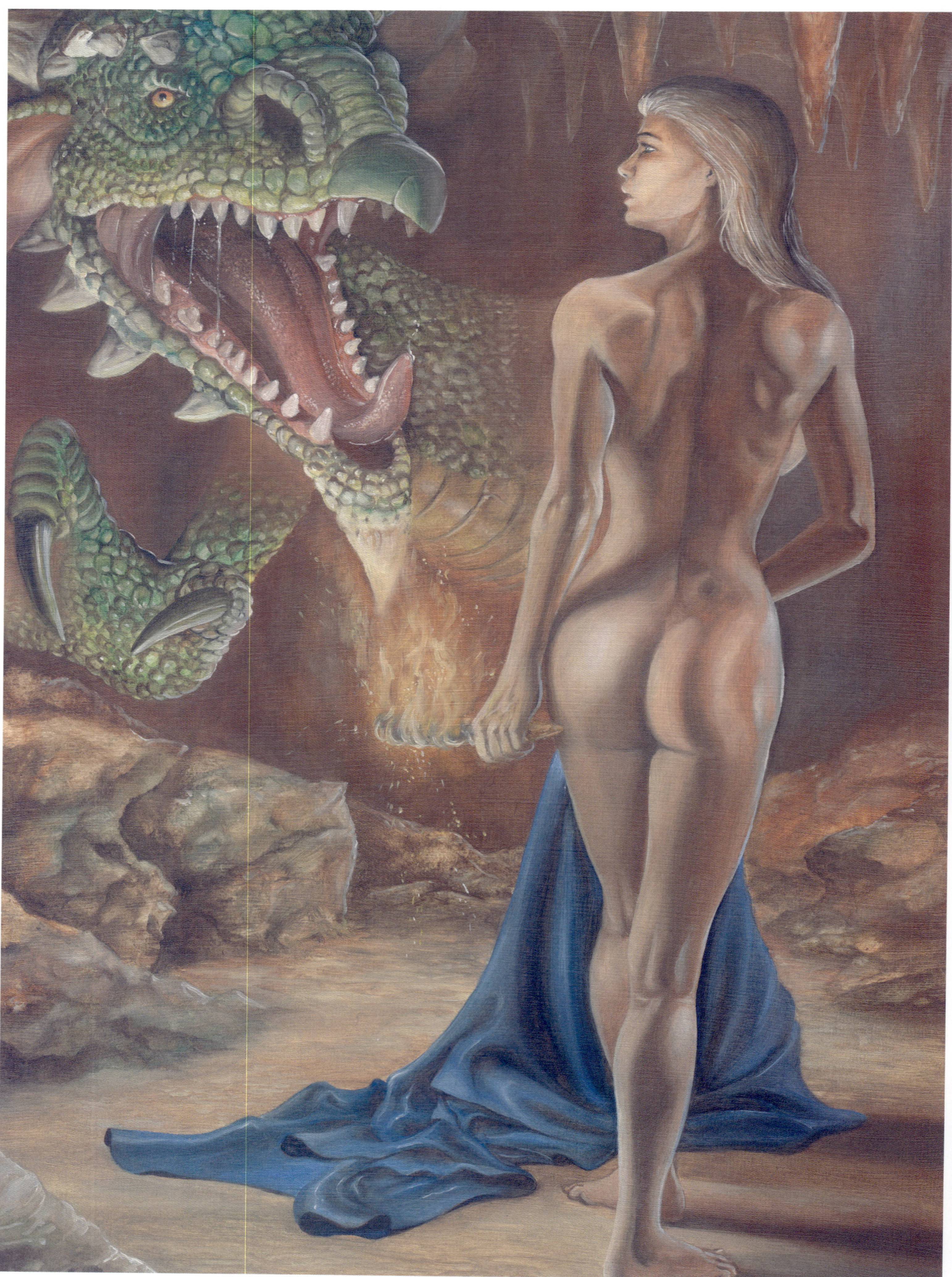

Diego Florio

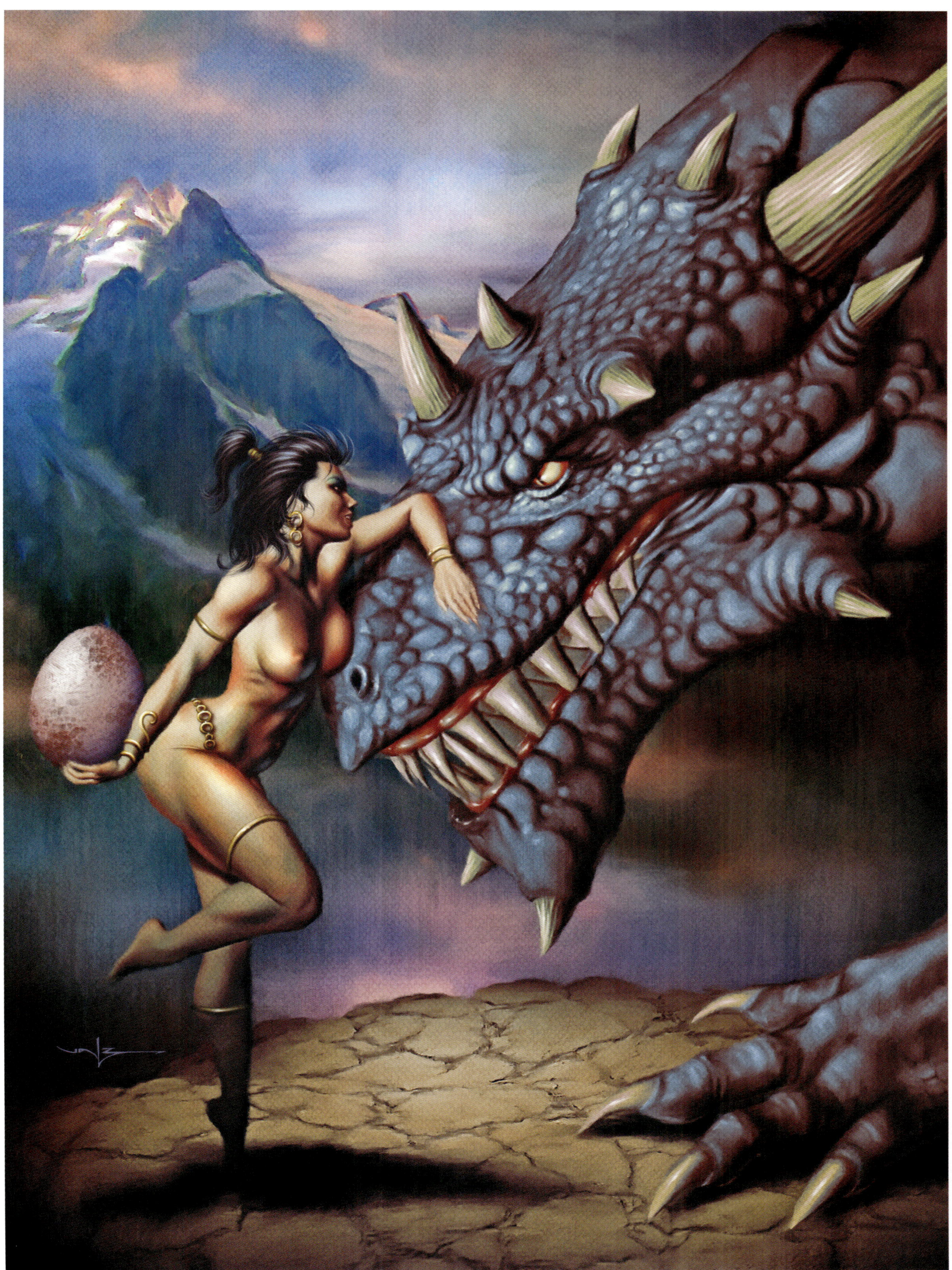

Carlos Valenzuela

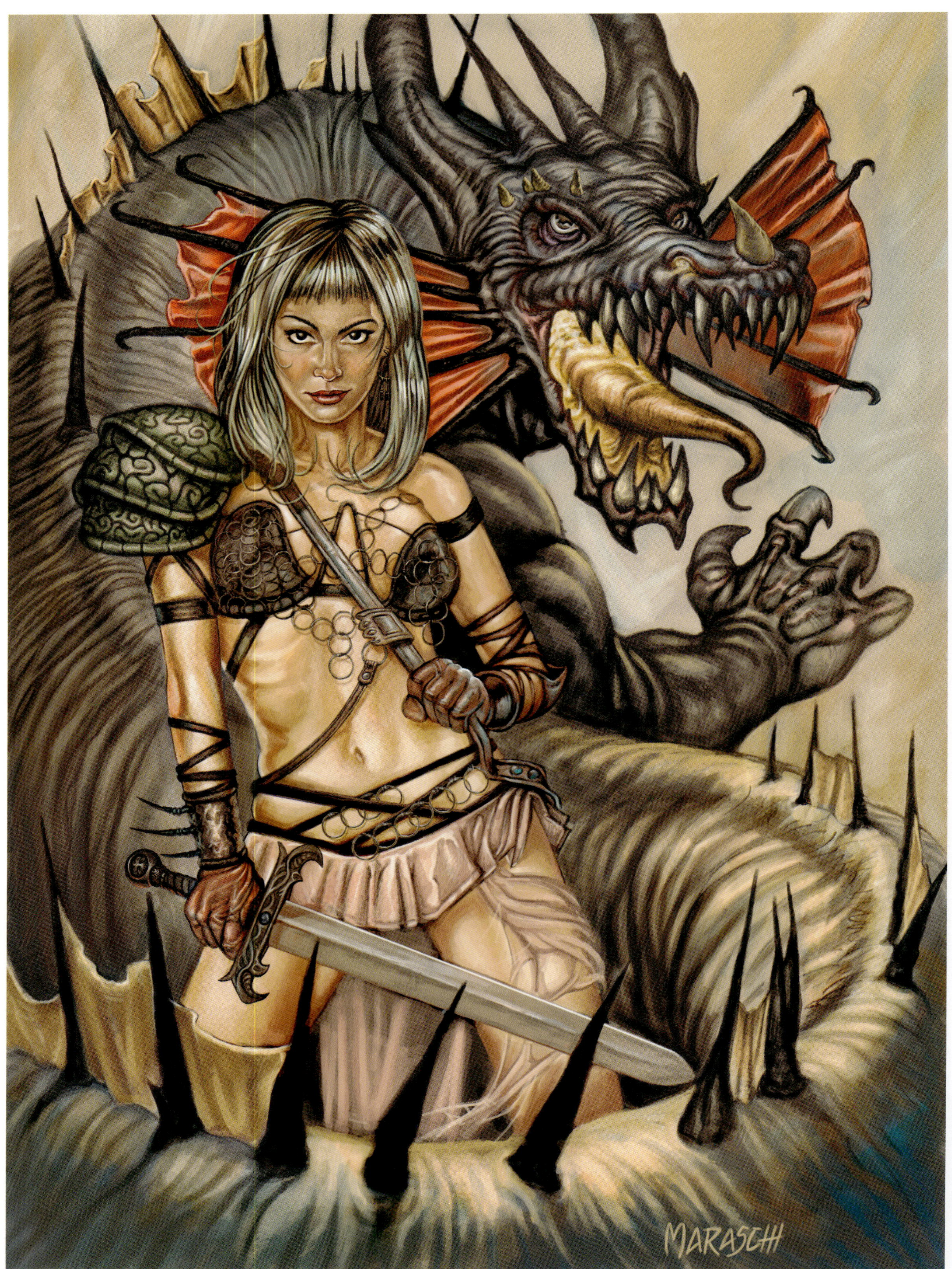

Anibal Maraschi

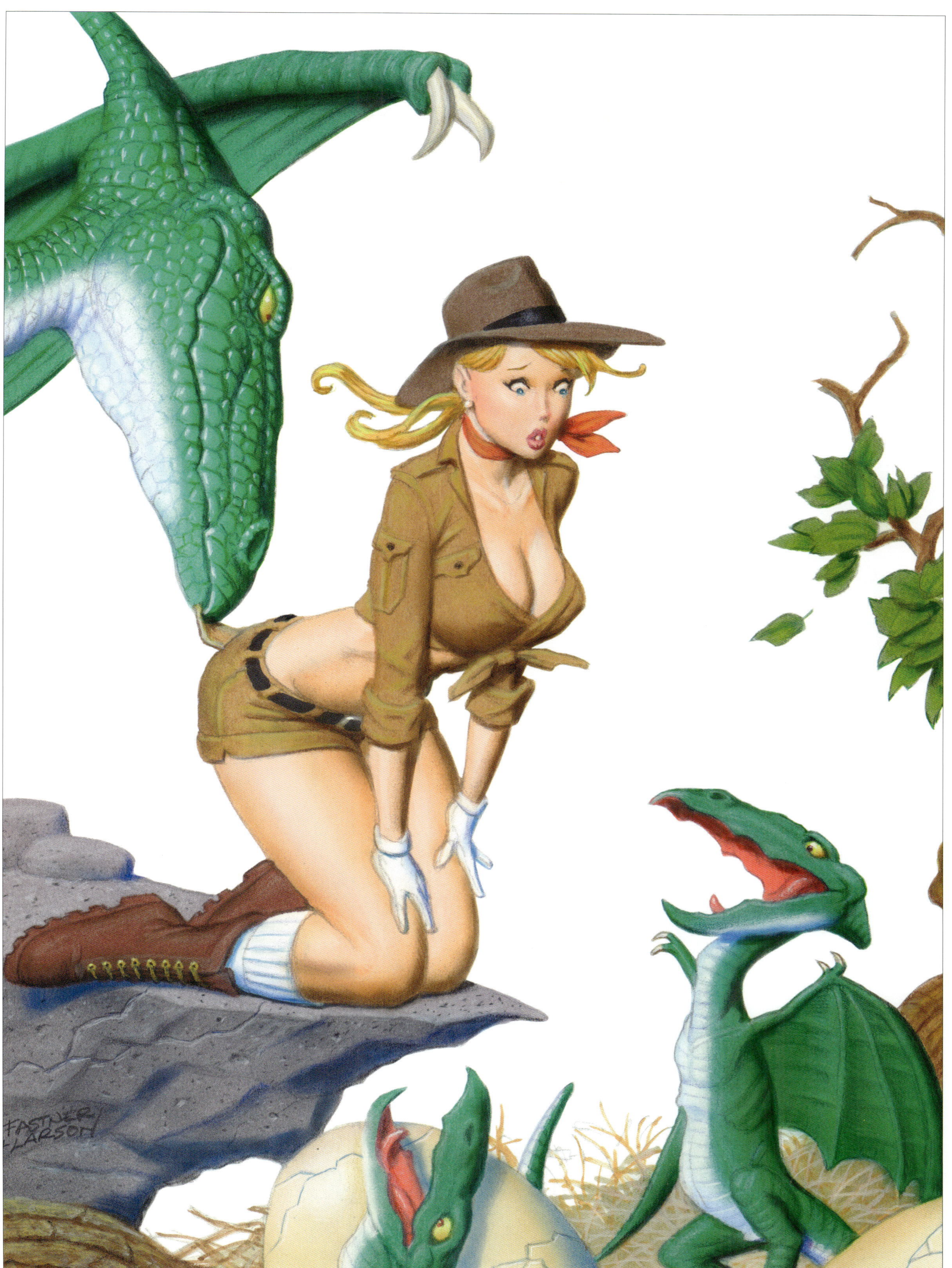

Steve Fastner & Rich Larson

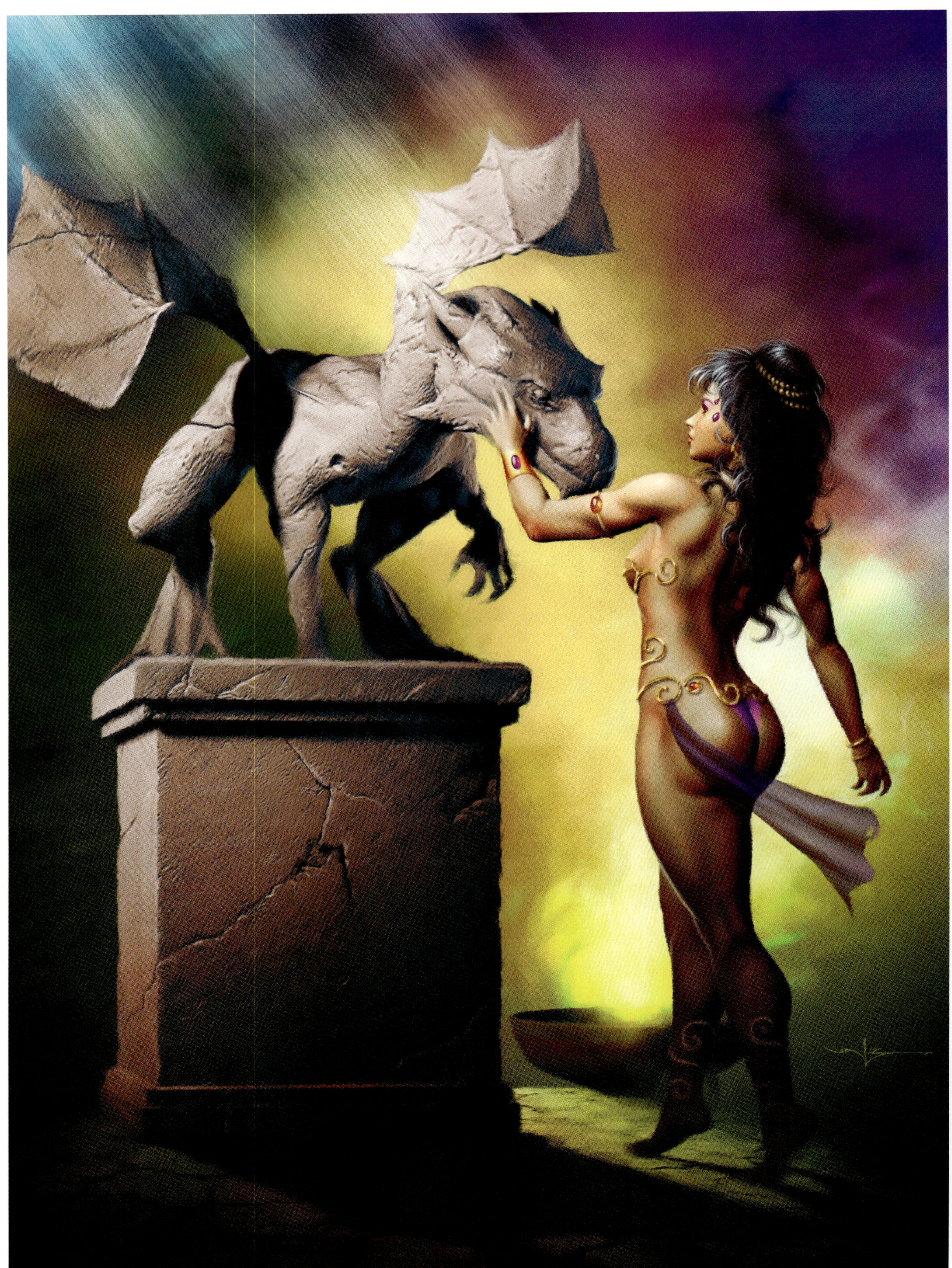

Carlos Valenzuela

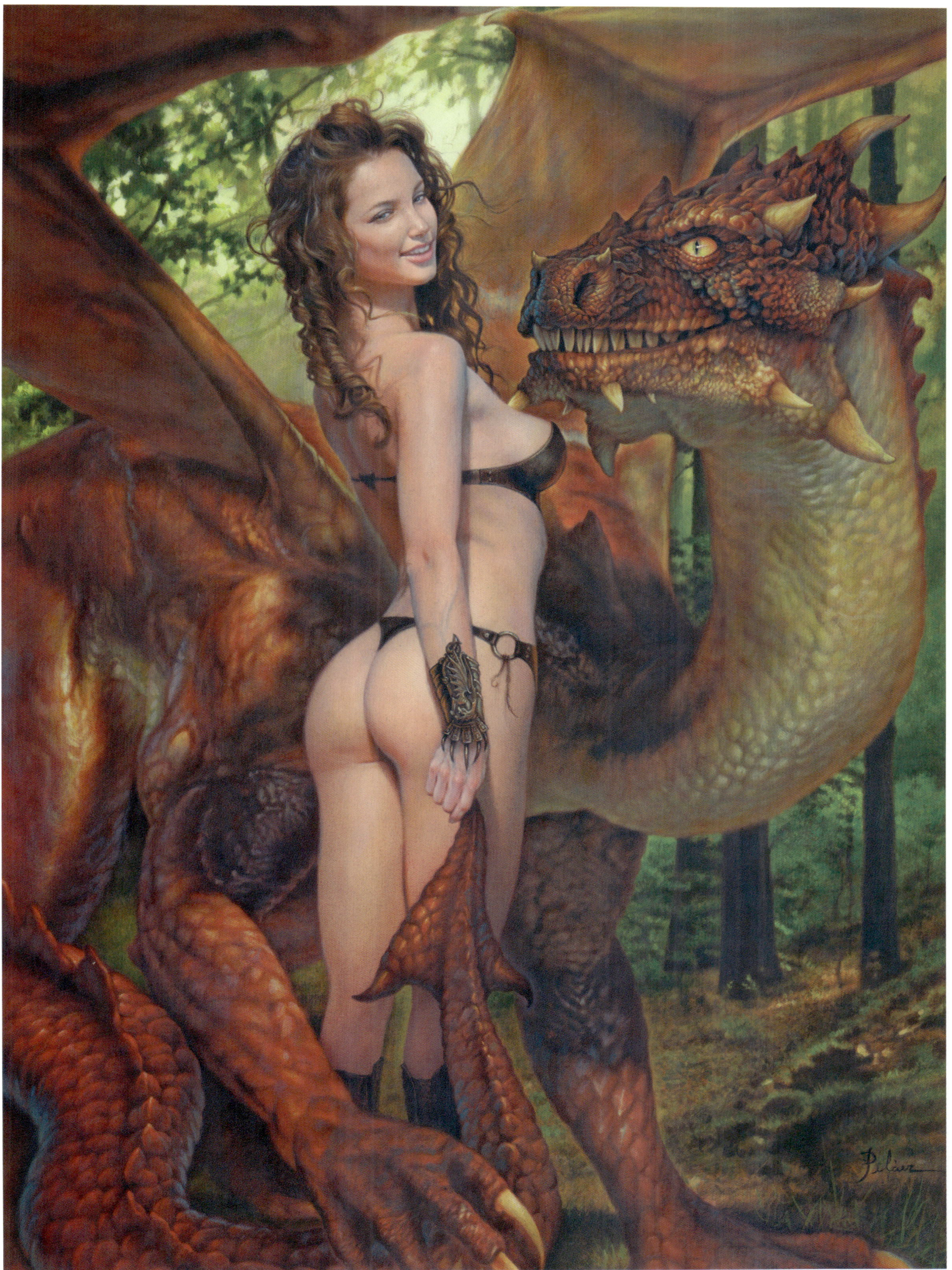

Pelaez

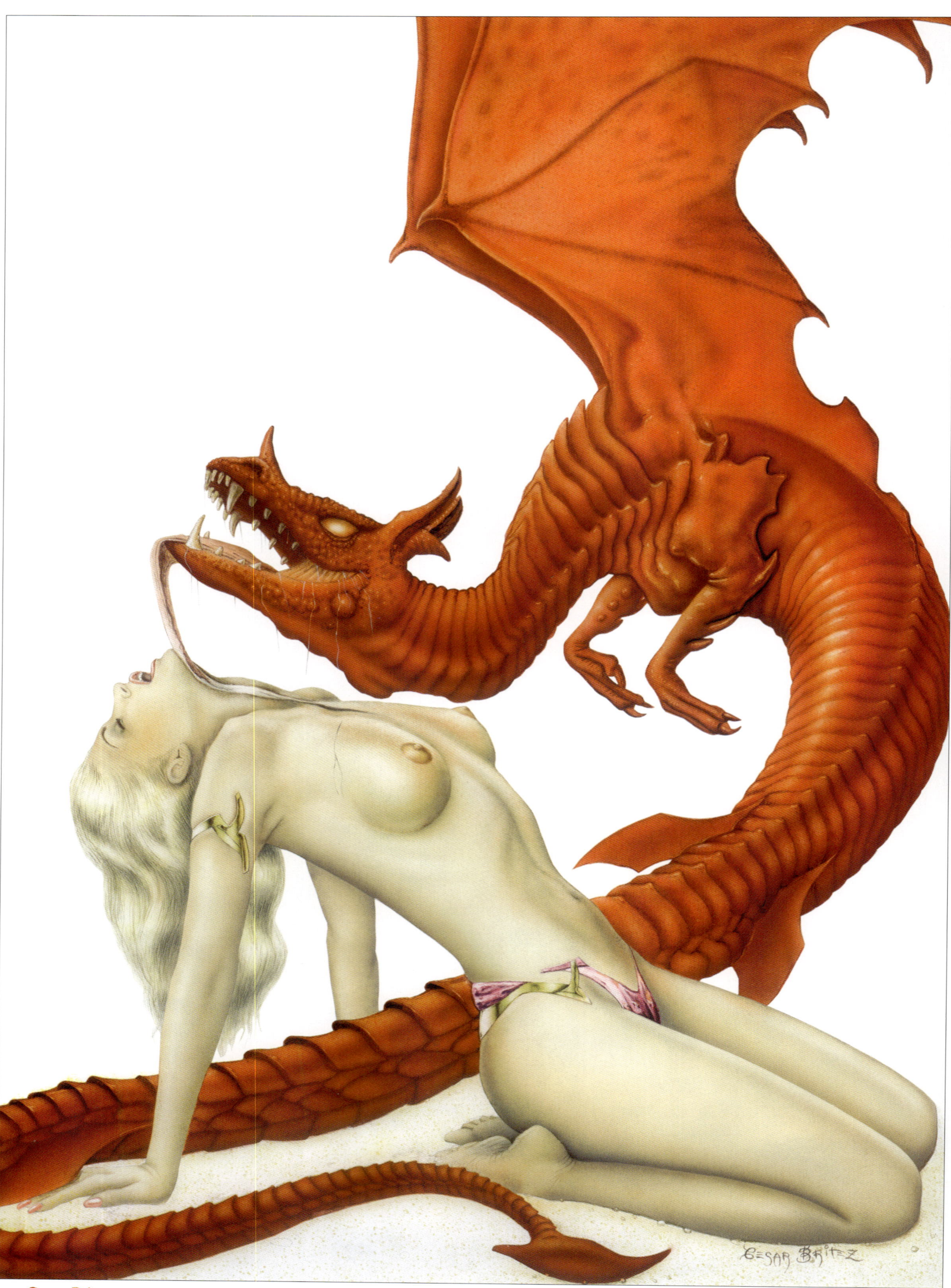

Cesar Britez

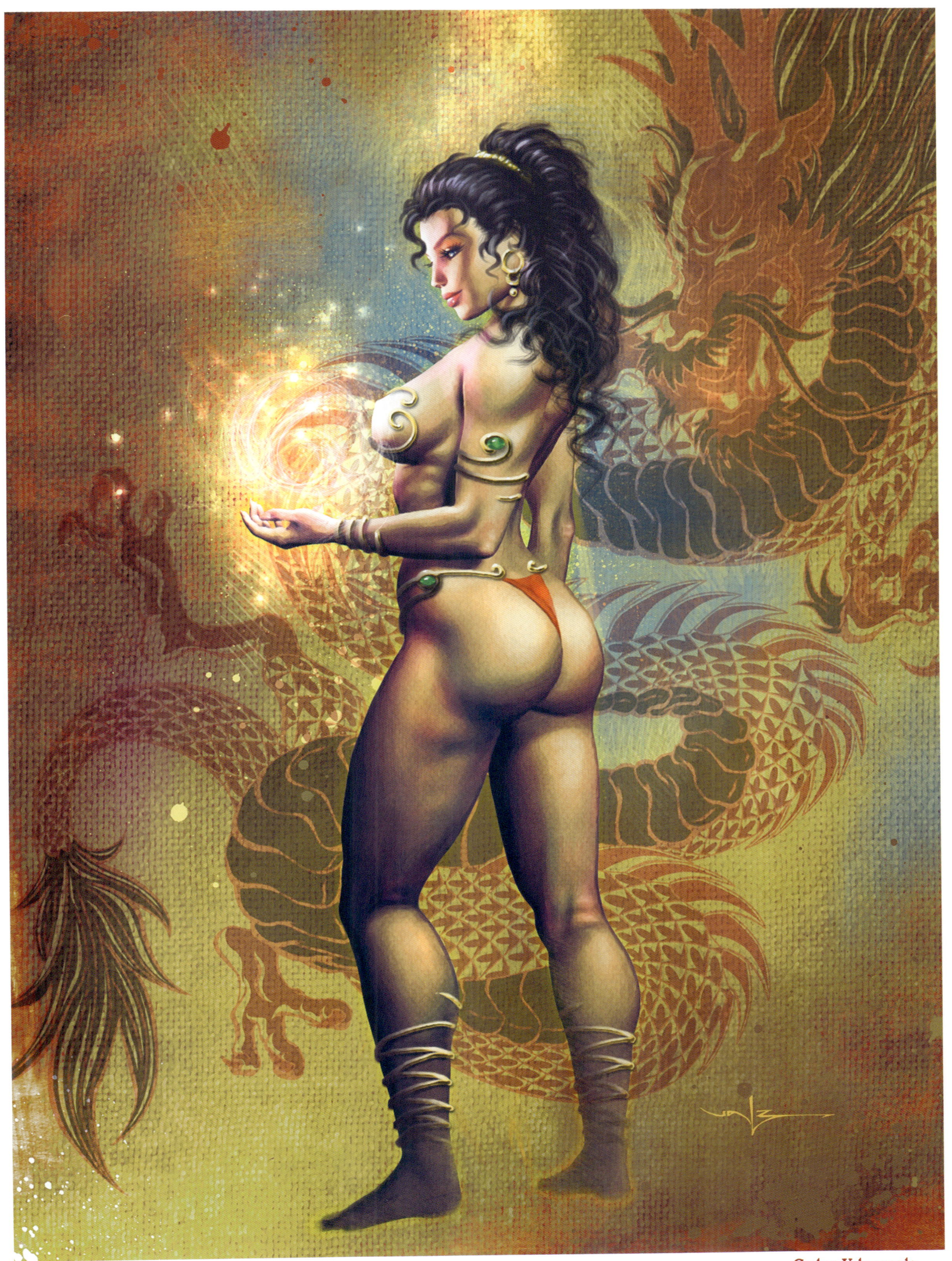

Carlos Valenzuela

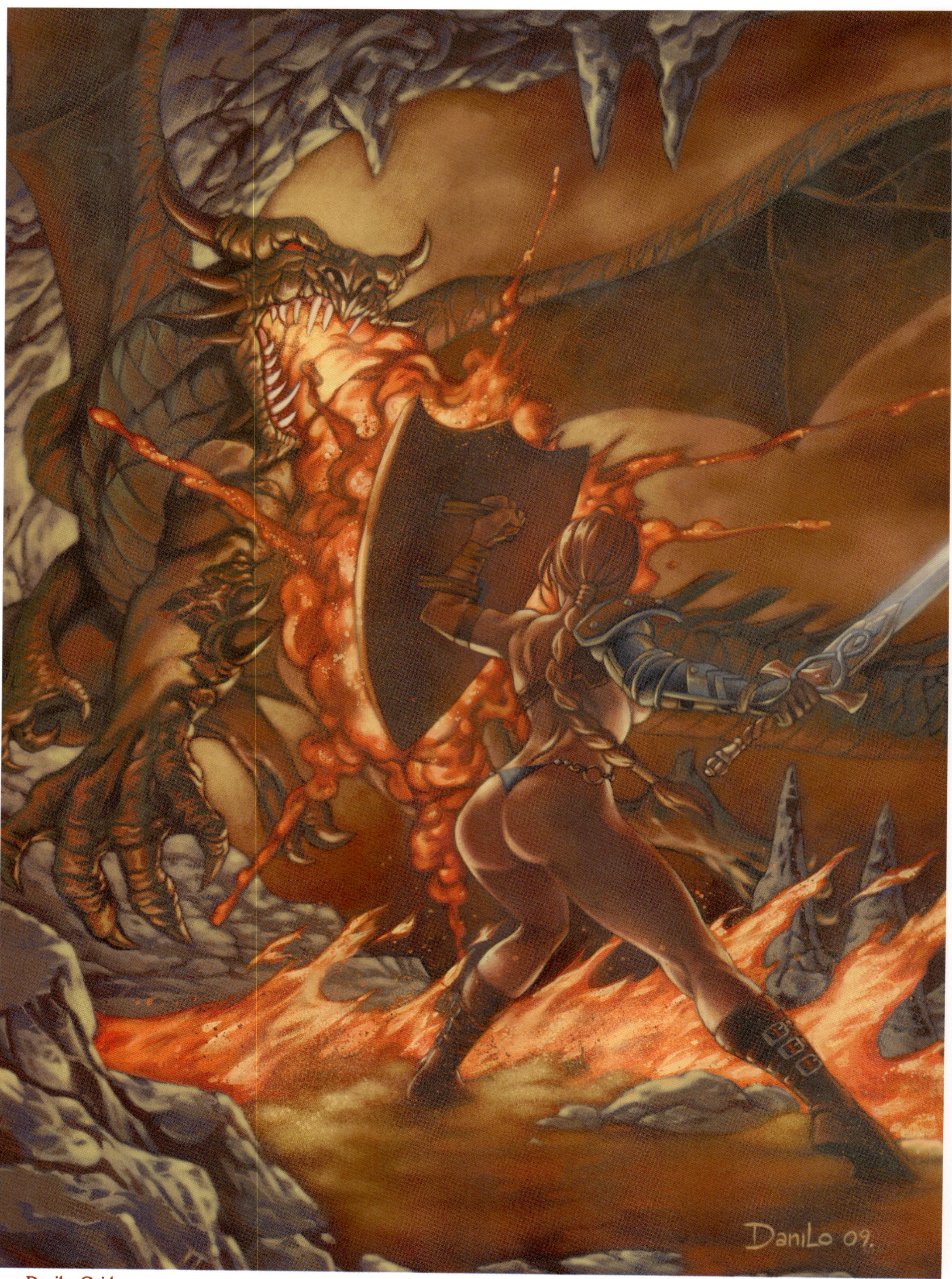

Danilo Guida

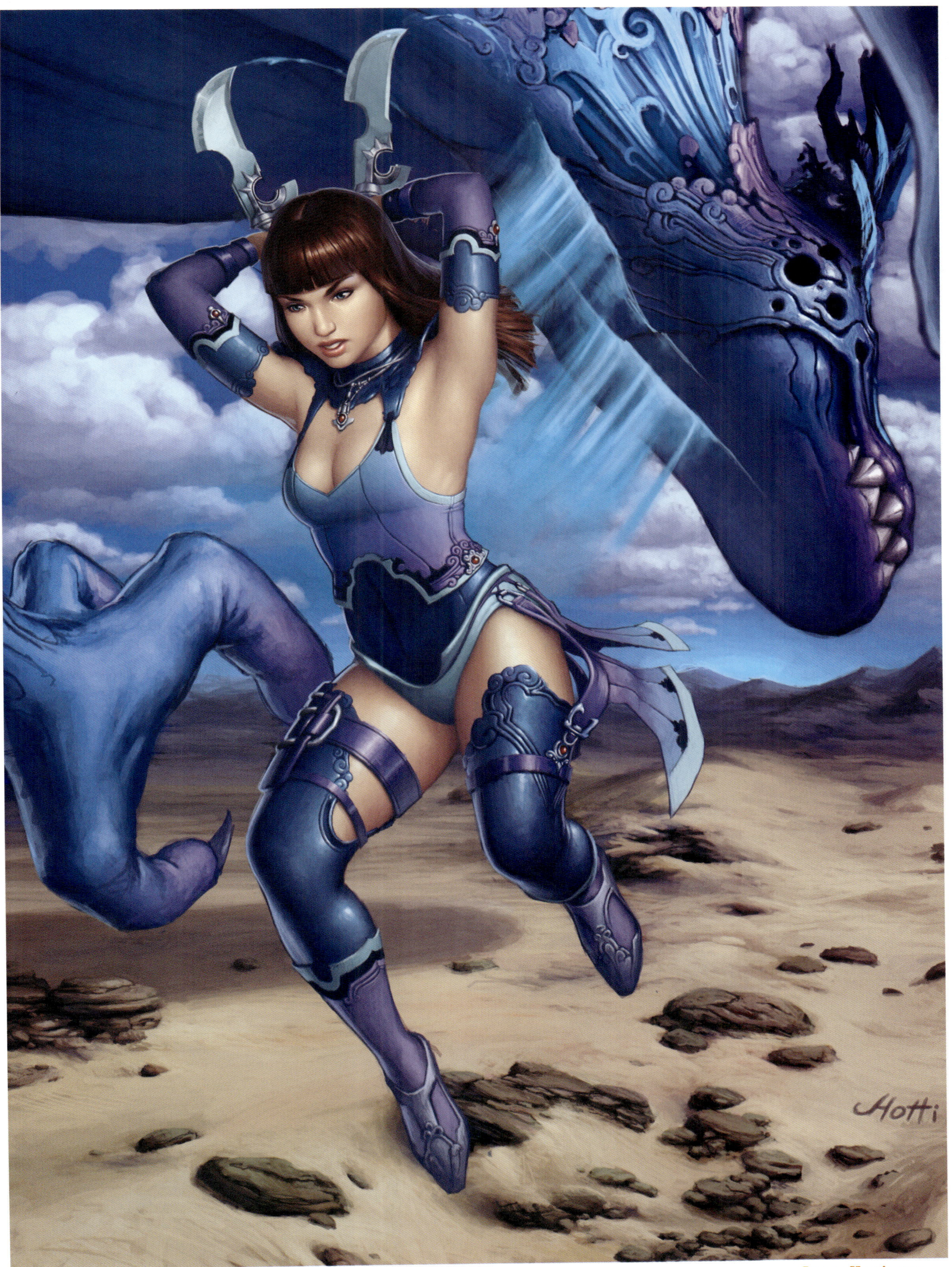

James Hottinger

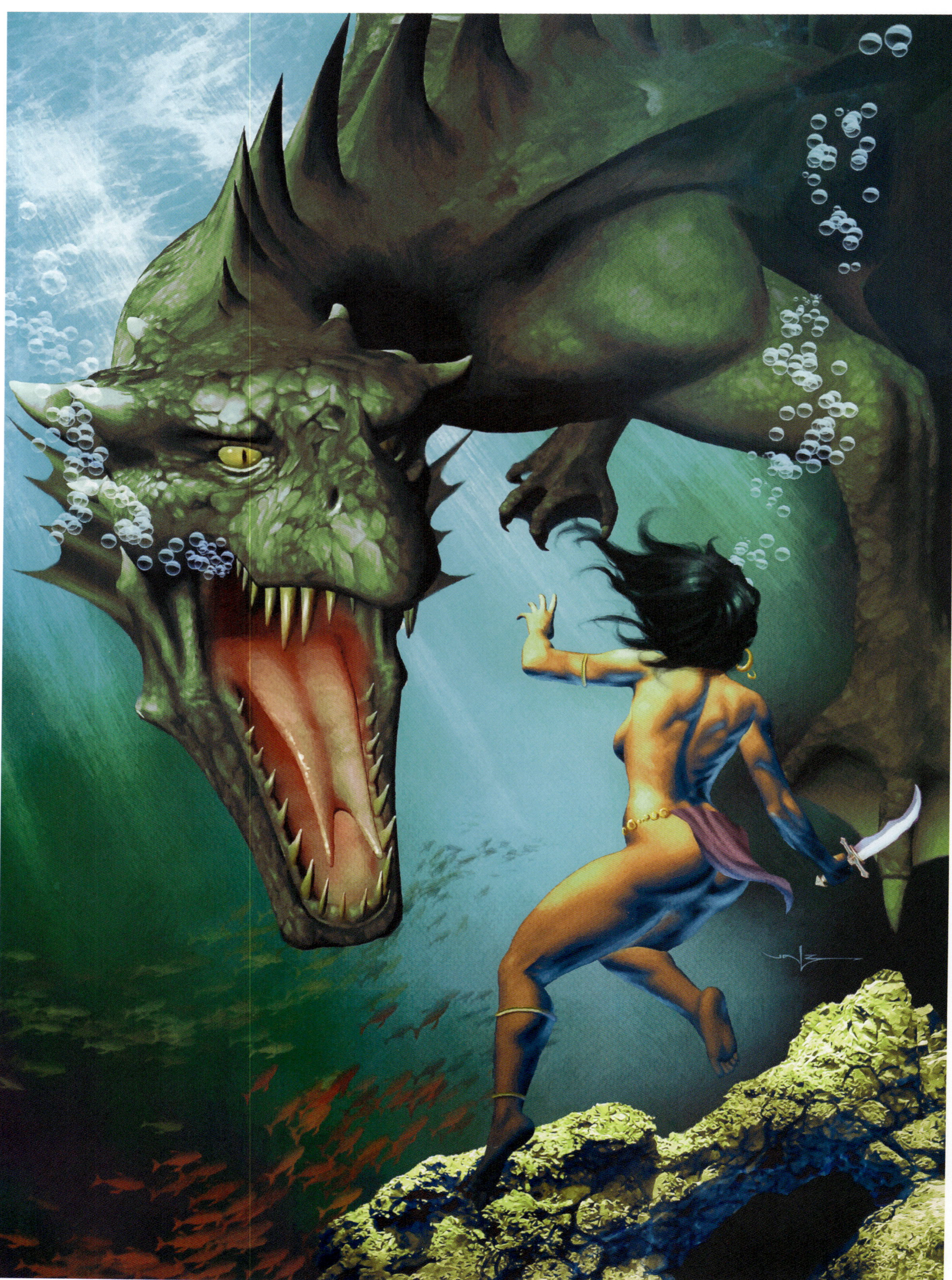

Carlos Valenzuela

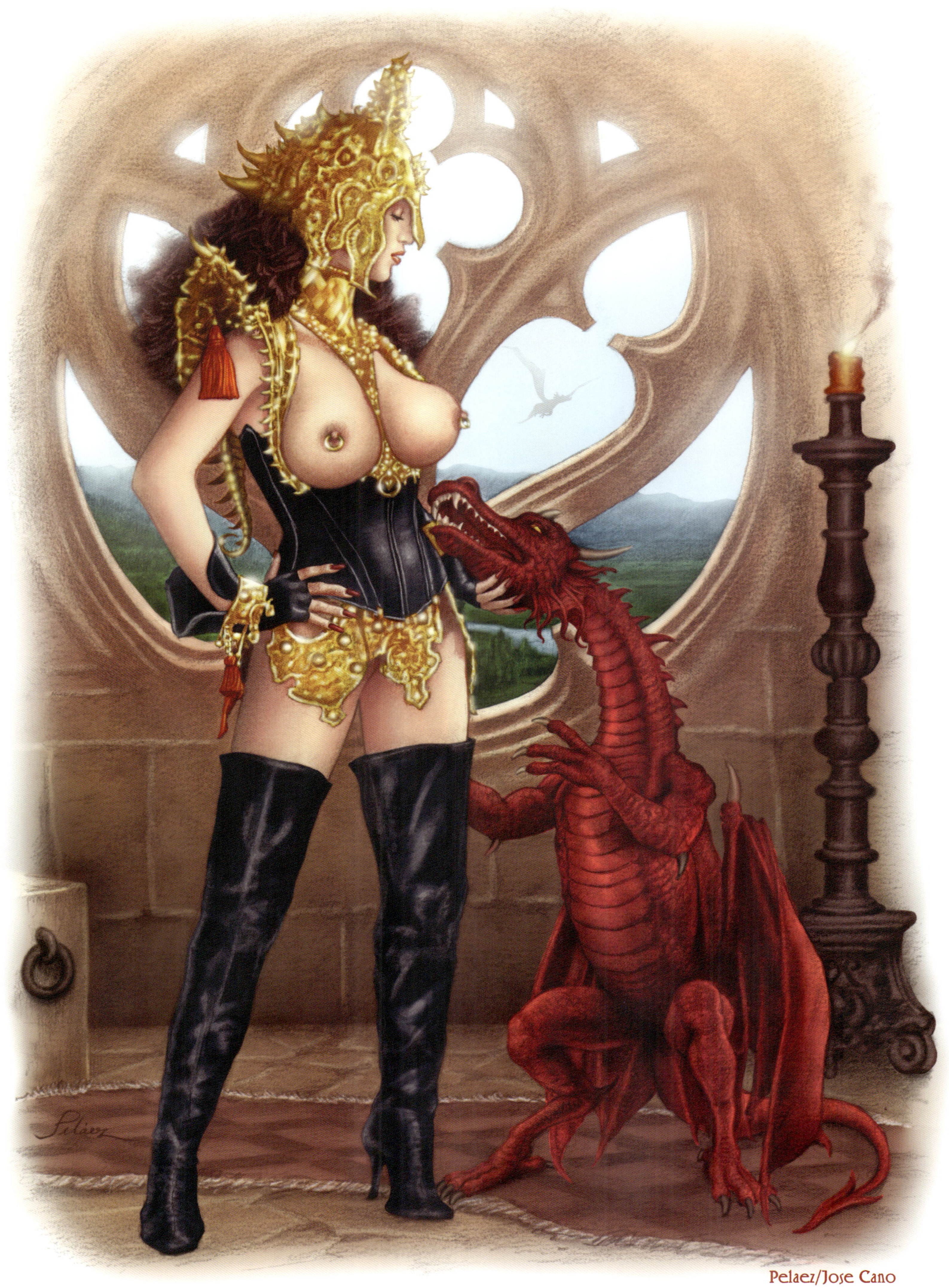

Pelaez/Jose Cano

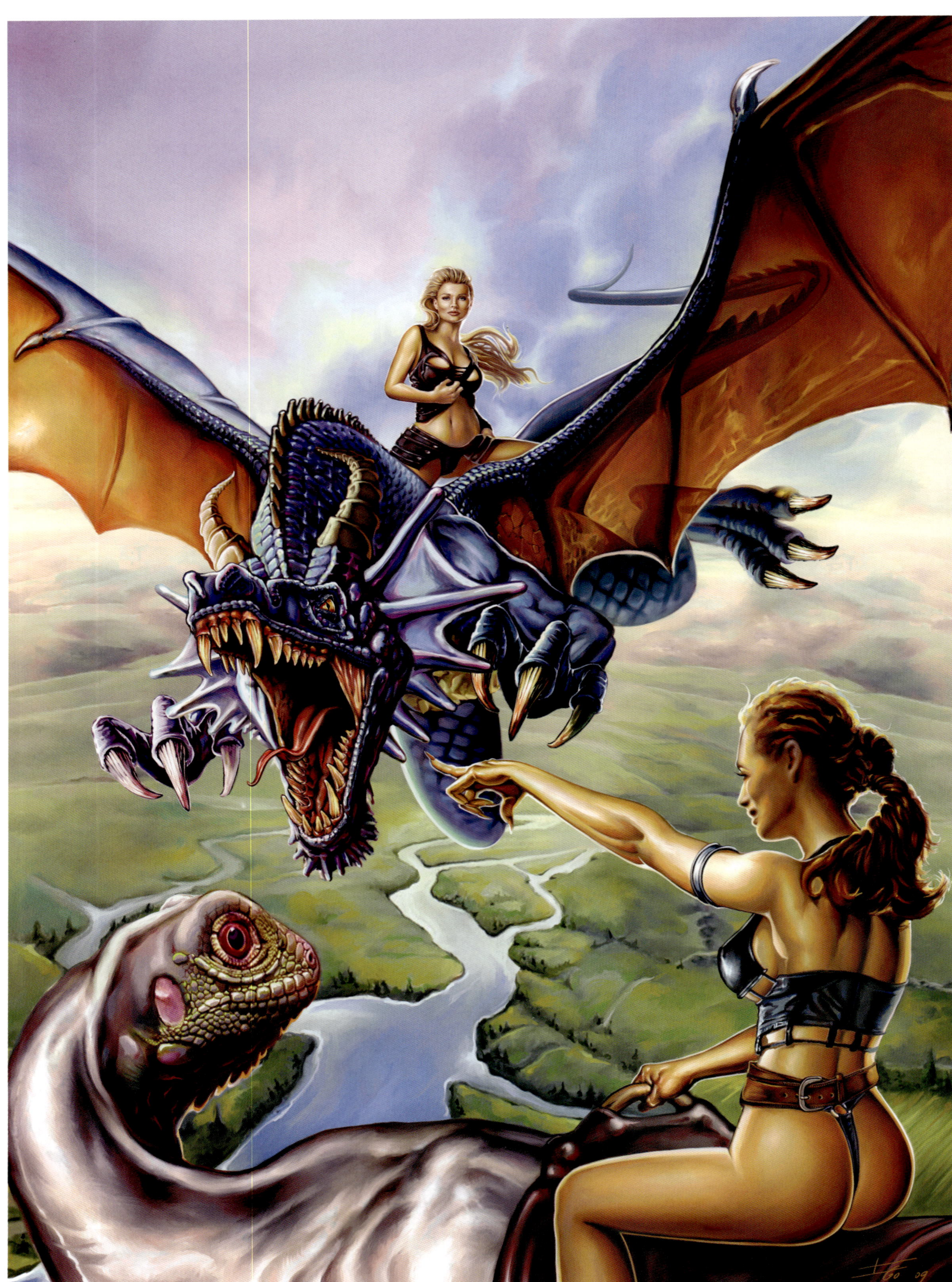

Inaki Ormaetxea

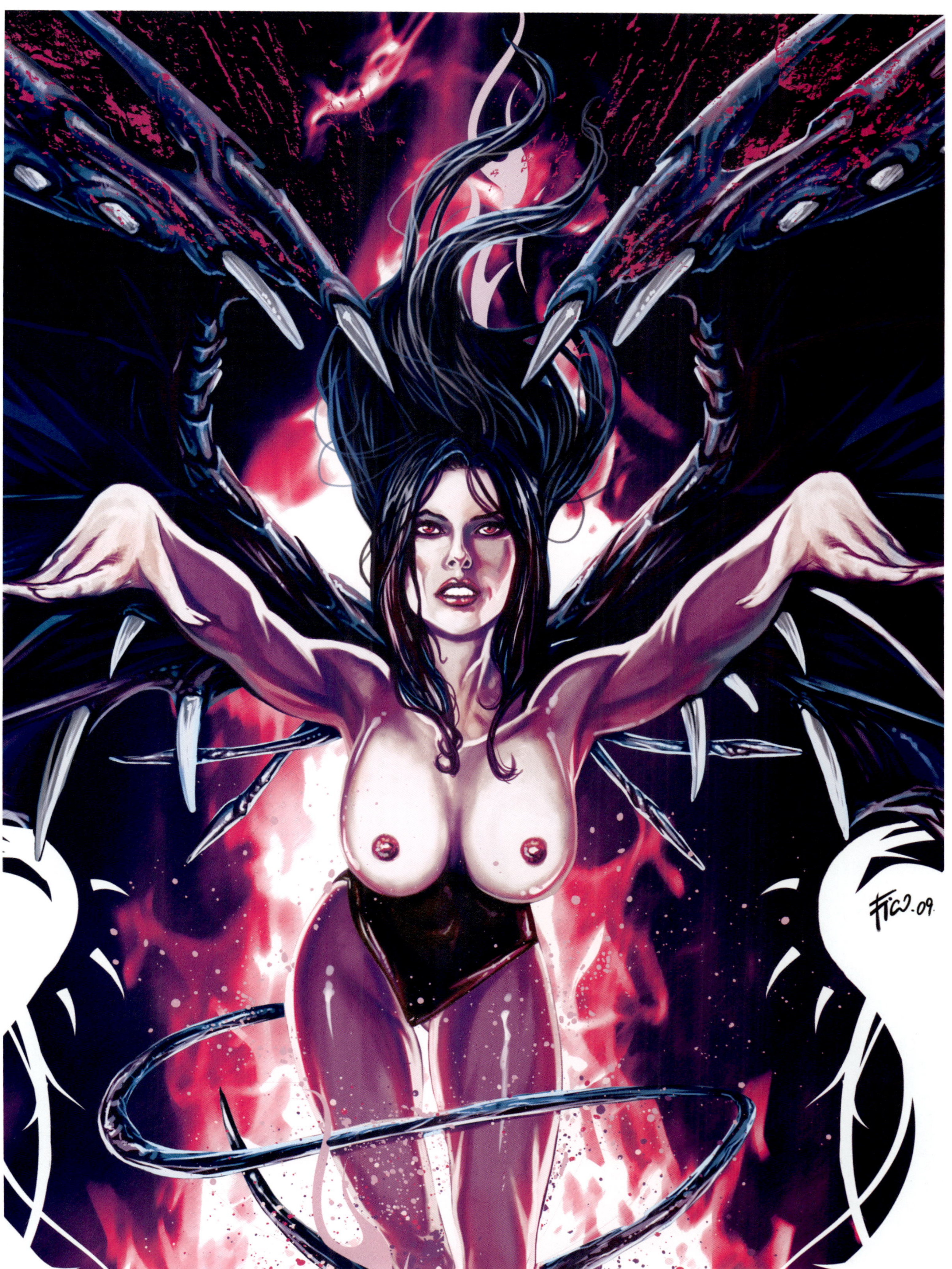

Federico Ossio

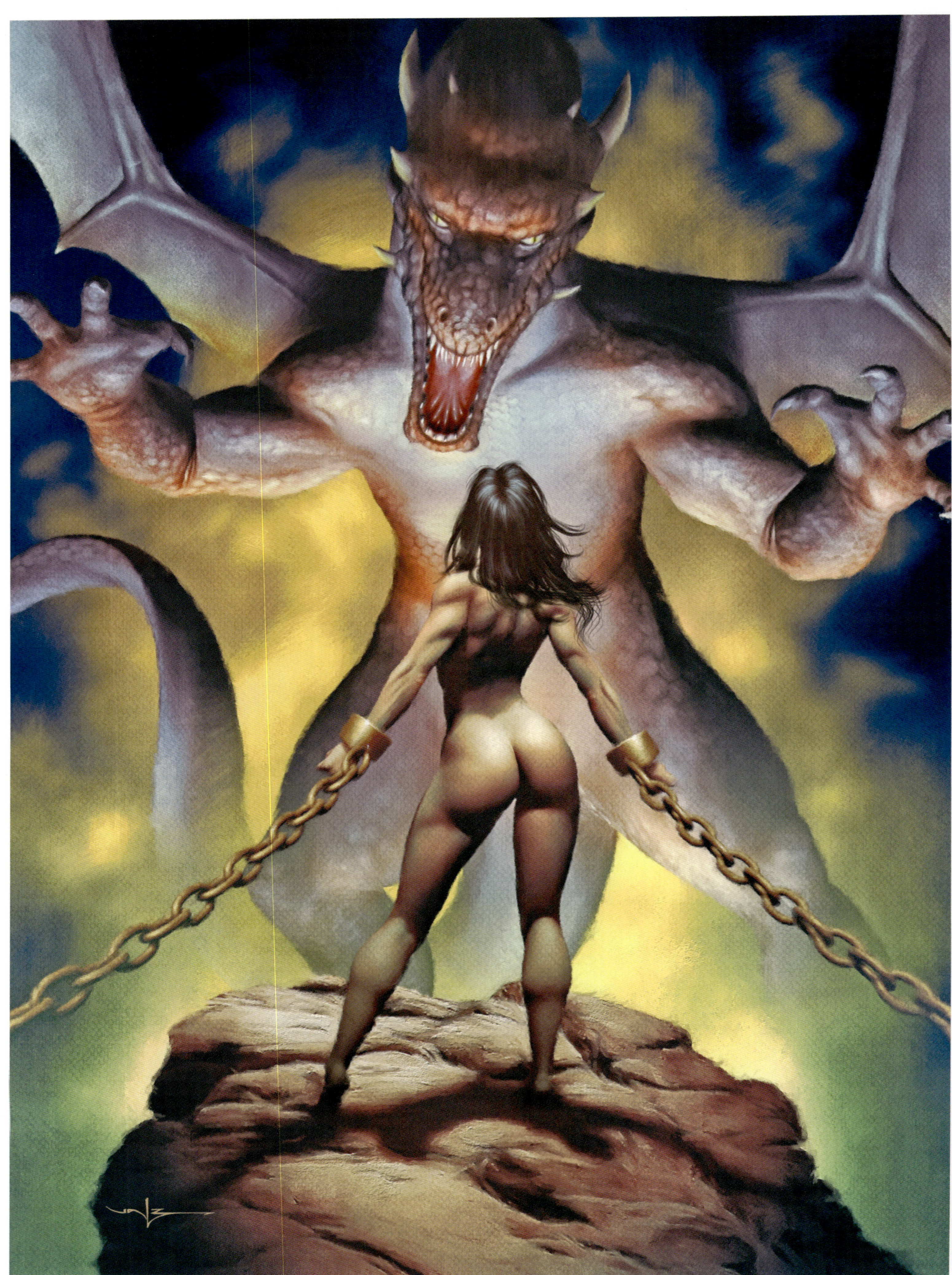

Carlos Valenzuela